Sylvia Plath

a reference guide
1973-1988

A
Reference
Guide
to
Literature

Ronald Gottesman
Editor

Sylvia Plath

a reference guide
1973-1988

SHERYL L. MEYERING

G.K.HALL&CO.
70 LINCOLN STREET, BOSTON, MASS.

Library of Congress Cataloging-in-Publication Data

Meyering, Sheryl L., 1948-
Sylvia Plath: a reference guide, 1973-1988 / Sheryl L. Meyering.
  p. cm. -- (A Reference guide to literature)
Includes bibliographical references.
ISBN 0-8161-8929-3
1. Plath, Sylvia--Bibliography. I. Title. II. Series.
Z8695.85.M49 1989
[PS3566.L27]   89-39238
016.811'54--dc20   CIP

This publication is printed on permanent/durable acid-free paper
MANUFACTURED IN THE UNITED STATES OF AMERICA

To my mother and father,
Jack and Virginia Meyering

Contents

The Author

Sheryl L. Meyering teaches American literature and Women's Studies at Southern Illinois University at Edwardsville. She has recently edited a book of critical essays on Charlotte Perkins Gilman, entitled *Charlotte Perkins Gilman: The Woman and Her Work* (1989). She is currently working on a study of Willa Cather's short fiction.

To the Reader

In 1974, G.K. Hall & Co. published *Sylvia Plath and Anne Sexton: A Reference Guide* by Cameron Northouse and Thomas P. Walsh. Since the section on Plath in that book contained criticism covering the years 1960-1973, I have not included those same citations here. I have, however, included in the appendix to this book all material from those years that was omitted in the earlier reference guide. Any article from the 1974 edition that has been reprinted after 1973 has been included here with an asterisk (*) after the reference number. The asterisk indicates the reference number from the 1974 publication, you should refer to that book for the original citation and annotation. Cross-references preceded by the letter A refer to the appendix in the present volume.

Introduction

Even as a child Sylvia Plath aspired to be an artist. From an early age, she had dedicated time and effort to her craft and garnered a good deal of recognition for it, mostly in the form of academic prizes and scholarships. When she was seventeen, her first work appeared in publications as diverse as *Seventeen*, the *Christian Science Monitor*, and the *Boston Globe*. Her academic and literary success continued throughout her years as an undergraduate at Smith College in Northampton, Massachusetts, which she attended on a scholarship and where she won nearly every prize and award available.

Unfortunately, Plath's driving ambition and perfectionist tendencies conflicted with a side of herself, created by the 1950s' view of women, that wanted to be popular with men, to have a date every Saturday night, marry, have children, and make her family first priority. These two warring sides of her personality eventually overwhelmed her, and during the summer following her junior year at Smith, after a stint in New York as guest editor for *Mademoiselle* magazine's college issue, she hid in the cellar of her mother's home and swallowed 50 sleeping pills. What followed was hospitalization, shock treatments, and a seeming recovery. Eventually, she returned to Smith, graduating summa cum laude in 1955.

Having won a Fulbright fellowship, Plath continued her education as a graduate student at Newnham College in Cambridge, England. There she met and fell in love with the poet Ted Hughes, whom she married in June of 1956. When she completed her work at Newnham, the two of them moved back to the United States, Plath taking a position at her alma mater teaching freshman English. The two poets were determined to devote more time to their own work, and when Hughes won a Guggenheim fellowship in 1959, they moved back to England, where they lived for a year in London.

By all outward appearances, Plath and Hughes were the perfect couple. Both worked seriously to perfect and publish their work. Plath's first major success came when her first collection of poetry, *The Colossus and Other Poems*, was published in 1960. Plath and Hughes also produced two children and moved to a country home in Devon. By the summer of 1962, however, the marriage was crumbling. Sylvia discovered that Ted was involved in an affair with a mutual acquaintance, and in early October Ted moved out of the Devon house. Sylvia remained there until December, when she moved with the children to a London flat that once belonged to William Butler Yeats.

By now, everyone who has ever heard of Sylvia Plath knows the rest of the story. In the early morning of 11 February 1963, she turned on the gas in the kitchen of her cold London flat and killed herself. The details of her suicide continue to intrigue and appall us: the towels she carefully stuffed under the kitchen door to prevent the gas from seeping into the bedroom of her two sleeping children, Nicholas, age one, and Frieda, nearly three; the cups of milk she left near their beds; the note she wrote, asking that the doctor be called; the nurse who arrived later than expected, too late to save Sylvia, who was already dead.

The manner of Plath's death had a notable effect on the critical responses to her work as well. Suddenly Plath's life was placed under a magnifying glass, and whatever details were discovered found their way into the subsequent assessments of her work. Linda W. Wagner describes the situation perceptively in the introduction to her recently published collection of critical essays on Plath's work:

> [After Plath's suicide] the second stage of criticism of her work began immediately. Within a week eulogies and laments appeared that, of necessity, changed the tenor of reader response for years to come. For a young woman to kill herself at the beginning of a successful writing career posed an intriguing–and frightening–mystery. All kinds of equations between art and life began to be suggested. Had Plath written so personally that she had somehow crossed the boundary between art and life? Was full exploration of the creative process dangerous? Why would a woman with two small children choose to leave not only her . . . art but also those dependents? Controversy was rampant, and criticism of Plath's work would never again be untouched by biography.[1]

Although these questions were never fully answered, hundreds of articles and several books were generated in the attempt to address them. The critical debate centered around the question of whether or not Plath's work could stand on its own artistic merit, without biographical facts to support or illuminate it. If it could not, then her talent as an artist would have to be considered negligible and Plath herself dismissed as just another clinically depressed, or at least hysterical, woman who could keep neither her mental illness nor her autobiography out of her work.

The first serious critical scrutiny of and response to Plath's work, however, came while she was still alive when *The Colossus and Other Poems* appeared in 1960. At that time, critics did not have to deal with the perplexing questions raised by her suicide. While most reviewers emphasized the influences of other poets on Plath's style, especially Theodore Roethke and John Crowe Ransom, the volume was generally well received. Many critics noted Plath's devotion to form and control. John Wain, for example, in a review published in the 13 January 1961 issue of *Spectator* comments on Plath's meticulous construction of each line.[2] Howard Sargeant makes much the same observation in his review published later that year in *English*: "what few defects there are in this distinguished first volume are due more to her sudden descents into fantasy than to any failure of craftsmanship."[3] Bernard Bergonzi gives the volume and unqualified endorsement, enthusiastically recommending it "to those inquiring spirits who demand at intervals if there are any new poets worth reading nowadays."[4]

The only other book to appear during Plath's lifetime was her novel, *The Bell Jar*, which was published in Britain under the pseudonym Victoria Lucas on 14 January 1963, less than one month before her death. This time the author was often compared with J. D. Salinger, her novel to *The Catcher in the Rye*; the book's heroine, Esther Greenwood, was often called a female Holden Caulfield. These comparisons were not made disparagingly. In fact, though a few reviewers were ambivalent, most praised the work as a skillful, moving, even brilliant first novel. Laurence Lerner maintained that the author had "an almost poetic delicacy of perception."[5] Robert Taubman called the novel "clever,"[6] and the London *Times Literary Supplement* judged it to be a "considerable achievement."[7]

After Plath's death, the criticism of her work continued to be positive. The change that occurred in reader response was not that it became negative, but that the circumstances of Plath's life and death began to be taken into account in nearly every review and essay. While Plath's biography became an issue very soon after her suicide, it became most obvious after the 1965 publication of *Ariel*, the thin volume of poems that would eventually make Plath's name as a great poet. Almost without exception critics recognized the creative genius behind the poems. Here, they agreed, was an original, brilliant poetic voice. No longer did Plath remind anyone of Lowell, Ransom,

Roethke, or Hughes. She had come into her own, and the result was breathtaking.

In nearly every critical assessment, however, the subject of Plath's life was confronted. In a few instances her work was simply dismissed as too personal, too autobiographical, too pathological to be considered art. P. N. Furbank expresses such an opinion in a March 1965 review: "It is no good pretending that Sylvia Plath's is not sick verse. . . . [Her art], for all its power, is an hysterical bravado in the face of insuperable calamity."[8] Francis Hope comes to a similar conclusion in a review published the following month. She maintains that Plath's talent is questionable because the *Ariel* poems consistently foist the details of the poet's personal life upon the reader.[9]

Most critics disagreed with these assertions, but, ironically enough, their very disagreement required them to address the issue and thereby kept the controversy alive. Writing in the London *Observer* on 14 March 1965, A. Alvarez concludes that *Ariel* "has an originality that keeps it apart from any poetic fads. It is too concentrated and detached and ironic for 'confessional' verse, with all that implies of self-indulgent cashing-in on misfortunes."[10] M. L. Rosenthal, too, refutes the implication that Plath was "cashing-in" on the tragic circumstances of her life when he declares that she never "confine[s] the account of a poem to the interpretation of a purely subjective state."[11] Other critics openly described the dilemma created by the knowledge of the circumstances under which Plath composed the *Ariel* poems. In his review for *Agenda*, for example, Peter Dale admits that "[t]hese poems were composed in circumstances which, for a number of reasons, make criticism difficult. . . . A critic is almost driven to find them successful so that the immortality of the work may compensate for the tragedy of the death."[12] In spite of such difficulty, however, he concludes that the poems "are a major technical achievement. . . . They will be read forever, like Keats's *Letters*."[13]

In 1971 and 1972, Ted Hughes and his sister Olwyn, who are Plath's literary executors, published *Crossing the Water* and *Winter Trees*, two more posthumous volumes of Plath's poetry. By then, what had come to be called the "Plath legend" or the "Cult of Plath" was so recognizable to her readers that critics could refer to the "legend" without fear of being misunderstood. In a review of *Crossing the Water* for *Library Journal*, for example, Domenica Paterno begins by asserting that "[l]egend has created an image of Plath as the artist of suicide, mesmerized by her own art, driven to have life imitate art, and so killing herself. But perhaps to this should be added Plath, the artist of anomie, feminine in genesis but human in 'gender.'"[14] The central argument has thus been recognized and refuted in a single sentence. Indeed, the review goes on to praise the volume as one which "deepens Plath's reputation for the talent to capture, and hold unflinchingly, death's apogean cold."[15]

The critical acclaim that greeted *Winter Trees*, too, often included the tacit assumption that the audience was aware of the still strong and prevalent legend that had grown up around Plath and her work. By this time, however, the majority of Plath scholars agreed that her poetic talent was unquestionable, that she was a major twentieth-century American poet.

In 1971, the same year Ted Hughes brought out *Crossing the Water* and *Winter Trees*, Harper & Row published *The Bell Jar* in the United States. Even more than her poetry, Plath's novel captured the American imagination, and it remained on best-seller lists for several weeks. Because these publications whetted the reading public's appetite for more information about Plath, a new subject began to creep into articles about her work. Almost in unison, critics and reviewers began to ask the same question: Why is Plath's work published in such an erratic manner? How is it that ten years after her death Plath's collected works, or at least her collected poems have not yet appeared? Increasingly, Ted Hughes's name appeared in the criticism, with the tone sometimes accusatory and sarcastic. The consensus was that as executor of his late wife's literary estate, he had what amounted to an obligation to make all of Plath's work available in a single volume.

Some of the anger expressed was very pointed, indeed. Jan B. Gordon's review of *Winter Trees* for *Modern Poetry Studies*, for example, includes this rather bitter observation: "We are now in the midst of a Sylvia Plath myth, a veritable saint's life whose relics Ted Hughes brings out every year or so for our communal worship in the role of editor-historian-biographer who has the keys to the kingdom."[16] Another reviewer, writing anonymously in the *Times Literary Supplement*, begins by asserting that "[t]he posthumous publication of Sylvia Plath's poems has been an oddly ill-organized affair. . . . How many poems are yet to come and from which period, is anybody's guess; but perhaps it's time to forget publishing logistics and produce a definitive, chronologically ordered collection."[17] The frustration so evident here was due in large part to the fact that Plath's readers were unable to assess her development as a writer accurately without access to the whole body of her work, arranged chronologically according to the date of composition.

Finally, suspicions about Hughes's private motives for his publishing decisions began to appear in print. In the 3 October 1971 *Observer*, A. Alvarez voices what many others had clearly been thinking when he speculates that one of Hughes's reasons for delaying an edition of Plath's collected work could be financial.[18] The next year, Eric Homberger elaborates on the same suspicion by offering information about just how profitable, in exact pounds and pence, these separate, thin editions of Plath's poems were in England alone. In an article published in *New Statesman*, Homberger decries the "proliferation of collectors' editions [of Plath's work, which has begun] to look like a bibliographic striptease of uncertain benefit to anyone other than the very wealthy."[19] The figures he assembles to support this contention are worth quoting here at length:

> The first of the collectors' editions, *Uncollected Poems,* appeared in 1965. ... Containing 11 poems, it was an edition of 150 copies selling for £1.25. A copy went at Sothebys recently for £50. In 1968 Turrett published *Three Women.* ... There were 180 copies selling at £10.50. *Uncollected Poems* is reprinted entire in *Crossing the Water* and *Three Women* is included in *Winter Trees.* A third title was published by Martin Booth's Sceptre Press, *Wreath for a Bridal.* This poem was included in Plath's Cambridge manuscript, *Two Lovers and a Beachcomber,* and had been published in *Poetry* (January 1957). The Sceptre edition consisted of 100 numbered copies at £10 each, and five copies numbered in Roman numerals (bound in full morocco) at £18.

> The fifth collectors' edition [*Fiesta Melons*] was published in 1971 and contained nine poems of which one was previously unpublished. ... [It] was published in an edition of 150 numbered copies, the first 75 signed, for no apparent reason, by Ted Hughes selling for £7. ...There were two very welcome 'commercial' collections of Plath's verse in 1971. *Crossing the Water* and *Winter Trees* contain, between the two of them, 53 poems of which three were previously unpublished. While these two volumes were being reviewed, amidst some grumbling at the random and piecemeal way Plath was being published, two further limited editions appeared from the Rainbow Press, run by Ted Hughes's sister, Olwyn, who is also the literary agent for Plath's work. The first of these sumptuous volumes, *Crystal Gazer,* contained 25 uncollected poems. ... The second title, *Lyonnesse,* was published by Rainbow Press in May 1971.[20]

Despite all the understandable "grumbling" about "piecemeal" publications, however, Ted Hughes denied Plath's readers a collected edition of her poems for another ten years. Instead, what he did next was give Plath's mother, Aurelia Plath, permission to publish a collection of her daughter's letters. When that book, *Letters Home by Sylvia Plath, Correspondence 1950-1963*, was published in 1975, critics were once again confounded. Again, everyone was asking a single question: How could the writer of these letters and the poet of *Ariel* be the same person? Review after review made the point that either Sylvia Plath had a split personality or the self she exposed to her mother was merely a carefully maintained act, contrived to gratify her mother with the notion that Sylvia was an exuberant, healthy, extremely talented and successful all-American girl.

There was widespread agreement among critics on this point, as well as on the assumption that Aurelia Plath's primary motive for publishing the letters was to counteract Plath's bleak portrayal of the mother-daughter relationship in *The Bell Jar*. Mrs. Plath had, in fact, written to Harper & Row before the American edition of the novel appeared to urge them not to publish it. Several reviews included this information. Anne Tyler's *National Observer* review, for instance, maintains that *Letters Home* "was intended . . . as an antidote to *The Bell Jar:* a view of Sylvia Plath's brighter side. But what it gives us far more clearly is a view of a system of values in which happiness is a virtue, success is the only outcome possible, and perfection is the very least one can expect of oneself or anyone else. The person who emerges from *Letters Home* is so elated and so feverishly gay that it makes the reader anxious for her."[21] Erica Jong, writing in the *Los Angeles Times Book Review*, concurs: "[T]hese letters largely depict [Aurelia's] relationship with Sylvia as warm and loving (the letters are so cheery and upbeat, in fact, that one tends at times to wonder whether Sylvia's need to always show her mother how happy she was wasn't perhaps part of her problem)."[22]

The next Plath volume offered by Hughes was *Johnny Panic and the Bible of Dreams*, a collection of short stories, articles, and journal excerpts, which appeared in England in 1977 and in the United States in 1979. After the astounding brilliance and originality of *Ariel* and the rest of Plath's poetry, this, the first of her short prose available to readers, was disappointing. Critics generally saw it as a kind of training ground for her later, more mature and original work. Many reviewers wondered how Plath could have been so devoted to selling short fiction to popular magazines when her obvious genius lay in creating those luminous poems of hers. G. S. Fraser comments that Plath "was quite content to be accepted by the homely *McCalls* or the smart *Mademoiselle*. With the American desire to 'make it,' her ideal, till her poetic genius took over, was through stories and journalism to be rich, famous, and travel, while remaining a wholesome and nice American girl."[23] While most critics viewed the material in *Johnny Panic* as apprentice work, they generally praised it as evidence of her development as a writer. Melody Zajdel maintains that "Plath's stories stylistically show her direct movement into the writing of *The Bell Jar*. . . . Although Plath's short stories will probably not change her reputation from poet to proficient popular fiction writer . . . they are markers to understanding Plath's skill in her finished fictional effort.[24]

Finally, nearly twenty years after Plath's death and after at least ten years of complaining by critics, Ted Hughes edited, arranged, and published Plath's *Collected Poems*. The result was neither surprising nor unexpected. Critics and the general public alike were pleased and grateful. The volume gained nearly universal high praise and won the Pulitzer Prize for Poetry in 1982. The recognition was well deserved, for, as Linda Wagner remarks, "[t]he 274 poems in the volume show *why* Plath changed the direction of contemporary poetry. They prove repeatedly that a versatile structure – the poet's ability to reflect mood in every nuance of the poem, from image to single line to patterns of sound repetition – is more important than any prescriptive technique. And they show with even more surprising consistency how successful Plath was in shifting those structures, molding tone and pace and language to reflect the poem in its unique form-both tragic and comic."[25] Michael Kirkham gives another enthusiastic evaluation. In a *Queen's Quarterly* essay, he asserts that "Sylvia Plath's poetry is better – more accomplished, assured, original – than its current reputation; it stands with the best American poetry of the fifties and sixties."[26] Such high praise is echoed by Dave Smith in an *American Poetry Review* article: "[W]hat I feel in *The Collected Poems* ... [is] the crack and sizzle of lightning that Mrs. Shelley invited down to create life. We can no more turn away from Sylvia Plath than we have been able to escape the unnamed creature we, not Mrs. Shelley, dubbed Frankenstein and Monster, the monster we persist in regarding as Death."[27]

This "crack and sizzle" of "the best American poetry of the fifties and sixties" was followed by the 1982 publication of *The Journals of Sylvia Plath*, the last of Plath's writing made available to date. Frances McCullough, Ted Hughes's coeditor for *The Journals*, maintains that except for the poetry, Plath's journals are "her most important work."[28] Most responses echoed this assessment. The consensus of critical opinion was that the primary value of *The Journals* lay in its portrayal of a writer whose dedication to her craft compelled her to work unrelentingly at perfecting it. Walter Clemons, for example, recommends the book "to any aspiring writer, particularly to a novice who thinks of Plath as a special case – a star clothed in the glamour of suicide. ... The journals help us appreciate the protracted, hard-working apprenticeship that led to her final blazing utterance."[29]

Another common refrain was heard in many responses to *The Journals*, however. Ted Hughes was once again the target of many critics' anger for his heavy editing of the book. Several people thought that what he omitted was very probably more important to an understanding of Sylvia Plath than what he included. One of the most astute and pointed attacks was made by Steven Gould Axelrod in an article published in *American Poetry Review*:

Some time after her death, Ted Hughes destroyed one of Sylvia Plath's surviving manuscripts, and a second one somehow vanished. In the Foreword to Plath's published *Journals* he writes: 'Two more notebooks survived for a while . . . and continued the record from late '59 to within three days of her death. The last of these contained entries for several months, and I destroyed it because I did not want her children to have to read it (in those days I regarded forgetfulness as an essential part of survival). The other disappeared.'

What was in those manuscripts, the one destroyed like a Jew in Nazi Germany, the other lost like a *desaparecido*? Hughes tells us that together they contained the last three years of Plath's journal. I need not belabor the value of the manuscripts as historical record, since it is obvious. What may be less obvious is the literary worth of those lost and destroyed pages. . . .

One can reasonably surmise that in quality, the later journal entries were to earlier ones as the poems of *Ariel* are to Plath's earlier poems. . . . It seems likely that if the journal had been allowed to survive in its entirety, it would have taken its place as a masterwork, Plath's *Walden,* her *Writer's Diary,* her *Education.*[30]

Because so much of Plath's writing is unavailable, critics are still left wondering about the judgments they made in the past and about the ones they will be able to make in the future. As Linda Wagner points out, "There is a mystery about the Plath *oeuvre.* And rightly. Her journals of the last three years of her life are not available. Several collections of materials are housed in the Smith Library Plath collection, sealed until either the year 2013 or the years of the deaths of both her mother and her younger brother. Plath's last novel, titled *Double Exposure,* has never been found, though 130 pages of it – at least – were known to exist at the time of her death."[31] This amount of mystery and intrigue is compelling – almost irresistible. When the seal is finally broken on the Smith Library Plath collection, the line of people waiting outside the door will likely be long indeed.

Notes

1. Linda W. Wagner, Introduction to *Sylvia Plath: The Critical Heritage* (London: Routledge & Kegan Paul, 1988), p. 1.

2. John Wain, "Farewell to the World," *Spectator* 206 (13 January 1961), p. 50.

3. Howard Sargeant, "Poetry Review," *English* 13 (Spring 1961), p. 157.

4. Bernard Bergonzi, "The Ransom Note," *Manchester Guardian* (25 November 1960), p. 9.

5. Laurence Lerner, "New Novels," *Listener* 69 (31 January 1963), p. 215.

6. Robert Taubman, "Anti-heroes," *New Statesman* 66 (25 January 1963), p. 128.

7. "Under the Skin." London *Times Literary Supplement* (25 January 1963), p. 53.

8. P.N. Furbank, "New Poetry," *Listener* 73 (11 March 1965), p. 379.

9. Francis Hope, "Suffer and Observe," *New Statesman* 69 (30 April 1965), pp. 687-88.

10. A. Alvarez, "Poetry in Extremis," London *Observer* (14 March 1965), p. 26.

11. M.L. Rosenthal, "Poetic Theory of Some Contemporary Poets," *Salmagundi* 1 (1966-67), p. 72.

12. Peter Dale, "'O Honey Bees Come Build . . . ,'" *Agenda* 4 (Summer 1966), p. 49.

13. Dale, p. 55.

14. Domenica Paterno, "Poetry," Library Journal 96 (1 October 1971), p. 3141.

15. Ibid.

16. Jan B. Gordon, "Saint Sylvia," *Modern Poetry Studies* 2 (1972), p. 286.

17. "A World in Disintegration." *Times Literary Supplement* (24 December 1971), p. 1602.

18. A. Alvarez, "Publish and Be Damned." *Observer* (3 October 1971), p. 36.

19. Eric Homberger, "The Uncollected Plath," *New Statesman* 84 (22 September 1972), pp. 404-5.

20. Ibid.

21. Anne Tyler. "'The Voice Hangs On, Gay, Tremulous,'" *National Observer* 15 (10 January 1976), p. 19.

22. Erica Jong, "Letters Focus Exquisite Rage of Sylvia Plath," *Los Angeles Times* (23 November 1975), "Book Section," p. 10.

23. G.S. Fraser, "Pass to the Centre," *Listener* 98 (27 October 1977), p. 541.

24. Melody Zajdel, "Apprenticed in a Bible of Dreams: Sylvia Plath's Short Stories." In *Critical Essays on Sylvia Plath*, edited by Linda W. Wagner (Boston: G.K. Hall & Co., 1984), p. 182.

25. Wagner, p. 18.

26. Michael Kirkham, "Sylvia Plath," *Queen's Quarterly* (Spring 1984), p. 166.

27. Dave Smith, "Sylvia Plath, the Electric Horse," *American Poetry Review* 11 (January-February 1982), p. 46.

28. Frances McCullough, "Editor's Note" to *The Journals of Sylvia Plath* (New York: Dial Press, 1982), p. ix.

29. Walter Clemons, "A Poet's Rage for Perfection," *Newsweek* 99 (3 May 1982), p. 77.

30. Steven Gould Axelrod, "The Second Destruction of Sylvia Plath," *American Poetry Review* 14 (March-April 1985), pp. 17-18.

31. Wagner, p. 21.

Writings by Sylvia Plath

Separate Works Published in Great Britain

A Winter Ship. Edinburgh: Tragara Press, 1960.

The Colossus and Other Poems. London: Heinemann, 1960, Alfred A. Knopf, 1962.

The Bell Jar (under pseudonym Victoria Lucas). London: Heinemann, 1963.

Ariel. London: Faber and Faber, 1965.

Uncollected Poems. London: Turret Books, 1966.

Wreath for a Bridal. Surrey: Sceptre Press, 1970.

Crystal Gazer. London: Rainbow Press, 1971.

Fiesta Melons. Exeter: Rougemont Press, 1971.

Crossing the Water. London: Faber and Faber, 1971.

Lyonnesse. London: Rainbow Press, 1971.

Million Dollar Month. Surrey: Haslemere Printing Co., 1971.

Winter Trees. London: Faber and Faber, 1971.

Child. Exeter: Rougemont Press, 1971.

Pursuit. London: Rainbow Press, 1974.

Letters Home. London: Faber and Faber, 1976.

The Bed Book. London: Faber and Faber, 1976.

Johnny Panic and the Bible of Dreams. London: Faber and Faber, 1977.

Two Poems. Bedfordshire: Sceptre Press, 1980.

Two Uncollected Poems. London: Anvil Press Poetry, 1980.

A Day in June. Ely: Embers Handpress, 1981.

Dialogue over a Ouija Board. Cambridge: Rainbow Press, 1981.

Collected Poems. London: Faber and Faber, 1981.

The Green Rock. Ely: Embers Handpress, 1982.
Selected Poems. London: Faber and Faber, 1985.

Separate Works Published in the United States

The Colossus and Other Poems. New York: Alfred A. Knopf, 1962.
Ariel. New York: Harper and Row, 1966.
The Bell Jar. New York: Harper and Row, 1971.
Crossing the Water. New York: Harper and Row, 1971.
Winter Trees. New York: Harper and Row, 1972.
Letters Home. New York: Harper and Row, 1975.
The Bed Book. New York: Harper and Row, 1976.
Johnny Panic and the Bible of Dreams. New York: Harper and Row, 1979.
The Collected Poems. New York: Harper and Row, 1981.
The Journals of Sylvia Plath. New York: Dial Press, 1982.

Writings about Sylvia Plath, 1973-1988

1973

1   ABSE, DANNI. "Sylvia Plath." In *Corgi Modern: Poets in Focus*.
    Edited by Dannie Abse. London: Corgi Books, pp. 79-86.
    Explores the widely accepted notion that "poets must suffer to
produce" their greatest work. This generation has adopted Plath as its
"martyr-poet." Her poetry is "triumphantly durable" but "limited by
neurotic elements in her nature." In some instances she had total,
brilliant intellectual control over her painful material; at others, "her
vision remained too inward, too recondite. . . ."

2   BAUMGAERTNER, JILL. "Four Poets: Blood Type New." *Cresset*
    36 (April): 16-19.
    A review of *Winter Trees*, "a startling creation of richly violent
images and uncanny insights . . . black humor and bitterness." Four of
Plath's poems are analyzed as examples: "Three Women: A poem for
Three Voices," "Brasilia," "Child," and "The Four."

3   BOYERS, ROBERT. "On Sylvia Plath." *Salmagundi* 21 (Winter):
    96-104.
    Judges *Crossing the Water* to be superior to *Ariel* largely
because Plath's "hunger to use [her] perception and transform its
objects into something they are not" is resisted, and "the objects retain
their identities." Plath's only failures are those poems in which "the
hand of Roethke [or Stevens] is unmistakably heavy on the page."
Reprinted: 1988.10.

1

1973

4   BURNHAM, RICHARD E. "Sylvia Plath's 'Lady Lazarus.'"
     Contemporary Poetry 1 (Winter): 42-46.
          Observes that the reading of "Lady Lazarus" on *The Spoken
     Arts Treasury of 100 Modern American Poets* recording (vol. 17)
     "contains certain lines [omitted] in the printed version." The spoken
     lines are printed with the omitted print version lines in brackets.

5   DAVISON, PETER. *Half Remembered: A Personal History*. New
     York: Harper and Row, pp. 169-72.
          Records memories of Plath. She was "feverishly enthusiastic
     about literature and asked me hundreds of questions about publishing.
     . . . She hardly wanted to be asked to slip into my . . . bed . . . Her quest
     for knowledge was voracious: I felt as though I were being cross
     examined, drained, eaten. . . ." Plath tells the author the story of her
     breakdown and "expressed gratitude for the help she had had."

6   DONOVAN, JOSEPHINE. "Sexual Politics in Sylvia Plath's Short
     Stories." *Minnesota Review* 4 (Spring): 150-57.
          Examines in detail five of Plath's stories: "The Wishing Box,"
     "The Fifteen Dollar Eagle," "The Daughters of Blossom Street," "The
     Fifty-Ninth Bear," and "Johnny Panic and the Bible of Dreams." In the
     first two, woman is viewed as exploited and victimized. In the next two,
     male-female conflict is raised to "a mythic level" and ends in triumph
     for the woman. Finally in "Johnny Panic," man seems to triumph, but
     the victor really is the woman's vision of redemptive love.

7   EVANS, NANCY BURR. "Looking Back over Four Years: A Stu-
     dent's Approach to Literature." *College English* 35 (December): 240-
     51.
          One student's account of her own awakening consciousness as
     a woman in a world of male-dominated literature and literary criticism.
     Plath's *The Bell Jar* validated her impulse to relate literature to her own
     life and allowed her to recognize her "oppression and . . . to do
     something about it."

8   FERRIER, CAROLE. "The Beekeeper and the Queen Bee: Sylvia
     Plath's Poetry." *Refractory Girl* 4 (Spring): 31-36.

2

Focuses on the movement in Plath's poetry from the almost strictly autobiographical to a more universal expression or relevance. Traces the figure of Plath's father through several poems in order to show "how the destructive or repressive aspects of dominating male influence are consciously realized, and then exorcised or eliminated."

9 FRASER, G. S. "A Hard Nut to Crack from Sylvia Plath." *Contemporary Poetry* 1 (Spring): 1-12.
    Reports on a seminar group's discussion of Plath's "The Hanging Man." Begins by describing the men in the class as threatened, seeming to feel as though they were "being raped," while "some of the women . . . sounded like rapists." Considers each line of the poem and describes how the class approached the questions "What-is-it-all-about . . . [and] how-is-it-done."

10 HAMILTON, IAN. "Songs among the Ruins." In *A Poetry Chronicle*. New York: Harper and Row, pp. 14-16.
    Presents Plath as a poet to whom the imagination is a "sanctuary." Her readers should never "confuse the defeat of her life with the triumph of her art." That she saw herself as imprisoned in a bell jar is clear even in her early poetry. The problem for Plath is that she must find a way "to escape from its imprisonment into the sort of freely expressive self-awareness that poetry needs, . . . and yet still function as mother, housewife, villager, etc."

11 HARDWICK, ELIZABETH. "On Sylvia Plath." In *Poetry Dimension I: A Living Record of the Poetry Year*. Edited by Jeremy Robson. London: Robson Books, pp. 13-29.
    Reprint of 1971.B21*. Reprinted: 1974.7; 1985.10.

12 HARRIS, MASON. "*The Bell Jar*." *West Coast Review* 8 (October): 54-56.
    Calls *The Bell Jar* "a forceful depiction of [adolescence] in the stifling, hermetically-sealed world of the Eisenhower 'Fifties.'" The novel is successful in its attempt to connect the narrator's breakdown "to her social world." Reprinted: 1984.17; 1988.31.

1973

13   HIGGINS, JUDITH. "Sylvia Plath's Growing Popularity with College Students." *University: A Princeton Quarterly* 58 (Fall): 48, 28-33.
        Surveys Plath's popularity among college students both in and out of the classroom. Plath is most widely read by students who write poetry themselves and those interested in the women's movement. Young people often identify with *The Bell Jar* because the story reminds them of the "unreality of the temporary university enclosure."

14   HOLBROOK, DAVID. "Sylvia Plath, Pathological Mortality, and the Avant-Garde." In *Pelican Guide to English Literature*. Edited by Boris Ford. Vol. 7, *The Modern Age*. Harmondsworth: Penguin Books, pp. 433-49.
        Discusses Plath's work as a challenge to the "assumption . . . that the reading of literature is beneficial to the sensibility." Because of Plath's fascination with death as rebirth, teaching Plath may even be called dangerous. Her work offers both "true" and "false" answers to "the question of existence." The later poems "move toward a deep and anguished recognition of the ambivalence and agony of being human. . . . Other[s] . . . renounce human solutions, and take to those of hate and the anti-human."

15   HOWE, IRVING. "The Plath Celebration: A Partial Dissent." In Howe's *The Critical Point: On Literature and Culture*. New York: Horizon Press, pp. 158-69.
        Reprint of 1972. B12*, "Sylvia Plath: A Partial Disagreement." Reprinted 1975.13; 1977.24.

16   HURLBERT, JOYCE. Review of *The Bell Jar*. *West Coast Review* 7 (January): 82.
        Compares *The Bell Jar* to Sandra Hochman's first novel, *Walking Papers*. Both books are replete with poetic images of "the pain and anguish of a search for identity in the modern scene where freedom and love, hate and violence, all recognizably mingle."

17   KAMEL, ROSE. "'A Self to Recover': Sylvia Plath's Bee Cycle Poems." *Modern Poetry Studies* 4 (Winter): 304-18.

Explains Plath's bee cycle poems on the basis of the actual behavior of bees scientifically documented by Plath's father, Otto in his *Bumblebees and Their Ways* (1943). "The erratic way the bees respond to what they perceive as dangerous to their collective existence reinforces the way the persona deals with her precarious sense of being." Consistently compares and contrasts the personae's stances with the roles and reactions of the bees to their environment.

18 LEIB, MARK E. "Into the Maelstrom." *Harvard Advocate* 106 (Winter) 45-47.
Reviews *Winter Trees*. Plath is, as usual, in full control of her craft as she handles familiar themes: "the encroachment of death," the search for escape from mental torment, and "the pitiless cruelty of [the] world." Plath avoids the pitfalls of much other confessional poetry by refusing to be "self-indulgent" and by remaining true to her "commitment to . . . art" while dealing with "merely human" subjects.

19 LEVY, LAURIE. "Outside the Bell Jar." *Ohio Review* 14 (Spring): 67-73.
The author recalls her experience as a guest editor with Sylvia Plath at *Mademoiselle* in 1958. Reprinted: 1977.33.

20 LORD, MAE MASKIT, and STONE, CAROL. "Fathers and Daughters: A Study of Three Poems." *Contemporary Psychoanalysis* 9 (August) 526-39.
Studies three poems by three different poets: Sylvia Plath, Diane Wakaski, and Anne Sexton. Each is seen as providing "insight into the father's significance to his growing daughter." Plath's "Daddy" is the most intense in its expression of "love and pain."

21 MALKOFF, KARL. "Sylvia Plath." In *Crowell's Handbook of Contemporary American Poetry*. New York: Thomas Y. Crowell, pp. 245-52.
Takes issue with the theory that Plath "risked her life in the interest of her art." More probable is that "the last brilliant poems were part of her finally unsuccessful effort to subdue self-destructive impulses rather than a disastrous attempt to invoke them." Plath's

1973

ability to explore the depths "beyond the boundaries of the self" and yet maintain control is explored through brief discussions of all her major works.

22 MARTIN, WENDY. "'God's Lioness': Sylvia Plath, Her Prose and Poetry." *Women's Studies* 1: 191-98.
Calls Plath one of the first American women writers "to refuse to conceal or disguise her true emotions." In exposing her "aggression, hostility, and despair . . . , she . . . challenged the traditional literary privatization of female experience."

23 MEISSNER, WILLIAM. "The Opening of the Flower: The Revelation of Suffering in Sylvia Plath's 'Tulips.'" *Contemporary Poetry* 1 (Spring): 13-17.
Reads the poem as ironic because what one expects from watching an opening flower is a "celebration of life"; instead the reader is offered the "gloom brought about by pain and disillusionment with life." Plath uses flower imagery to suggest suffering.

24 MILLINER, GLADYS W. "The Tragic Imperative: *The Awakening* and *The Bell Jar*." *Mary Wollstonecraft Newsletter* 2: 21-27.
Compares the two novels. Concentrates on the similarities between Esther Greenwood and Edna Pontellier. Both characters, like their creators, were "victims of the double standard [both] in careers . . . [and] in sexuality." They fail in their search for identity because society has no place for them, "no identity except the one imposed on [them] as [women]."

25 MIZEJEWSKI, LINDA. "Sappho to Sexton: Woman Uncontained." *College English* 35 (December): 340-45.
Begins with a description of Dido as "a woman uncontained, . . . loose and unpredictable," then contrasts this image with that of woman as "earth-mother," found in ancient Greek and Hebrew literature. Plath's "Ariel" is discussed (especially on pp. 341-42) as an example of the former, which is a "much older, if less aggressive tradition."

26 MONTEITH, CHARLES. Letter to the Editor. *Times Literary Supplement*, 7 December, p. 1508.

Apologizes to Elizabeth Sigmund (see 1973.30) on behalf of Faber and Faber for having "careless[ly]" removed the dedication in their edition of *The Bell Jar*.

27 NILSEN, ALLEEN PACE. "Death and Dying: Facts, Fiction, Folklore." *English Journal* 62 (November): 1188.

Review of *The Bell Jar*. The book is not "better" because its author committed suicide, yet Plath's suicide undeniably "colors and adds significance" to the reading of it.

28 PROCOPIOW, NORMA. "Sylvia Plath and the New England Mind." *Thoth* 13 (Fall): 3-15.

Connects Plath's preoccupation with death in her poetry to the New England Puritan "tradition in which Dickinson, Melville, and Hawthorne also stand." Plath's star imagery often has "a strong flavor of doctrinal predestination."

29 RAPONE, ANITA. "The Body Is the Role: Sylvia Plath." In *Radical Feminism*. Edited by Anne Koedt, Ellen Levine, and Anita Rapone. New York: Quadrangle; Toronto: Fitzhenry and Whiteside, pp. 407-12.

Deals primarily with the *Ariel* poems as describing the constricted world of one woman which "speaks to all women." Because the persona is defined solely by her female body, she is "locked into a mere physical presence," trapped, vulnerable and controlled by others. *The Colossus* is discussed briefly.

30 SIGMUND, ELIZABETH. Letter to the Editor. *Times Literary Supplement*, 30 November, p. 1477.

Reprimands Faber and Faber for having removed the dedication from their edition of *The Bell Jar*. Plath had dedicated the novel to Sigmund (then Elizabeth Compton) and her ex-husband.

1973

31   TALBOT, NORMAN. "Sisterhood Is Powerful: The Moon in Sylvia
       Plath's Poetry." *New Poetry* 21 (June): 23-36.
           Traces Plath's use of the moon as a "major female emblem" in
       her poetry. The white face of the moon represents "female power
       mobilized against the male tyranny of father, husband, priest and all
       other black men." The moon image is compared and contrasted to the
       queen bee as a symbol of "the eternal female form divine."

32   UROFF, MARGARET D. "Sylvia Plath on Motherhood." *Midwest
       Quarterly* 15 (October): 70-90.
           Explores Plath's poems on the subject of motherhood. Since
       she wrote more poems about mothering than about anything else, her
       reputation as a death obsessed artist must be re-evaluated. Plath
       "breaks through conventional attitudes to explore her own intense and
       ambivalent reactions." The poems are discussed in detail.

1974

1   ASHFORD, DEBORAH. "Sylvia Plath's Poetry: A Complex of
       Irreconcilable Antagonisms." *Concerning Poetry* 7 (Spring): 62-69.
           Maintains that a thorough study of the "problems of develop-
       ment" in Plath's work is difficult because critics have tended to focus so
       much on 1) her suicide and 2) *The Colossus* and *Ariel*. Further, Ted
       Hughes has not published her work in the order of its composition,
       making a real tracing of thematic developments over time all but
       impossible. However, a close reading of the currently available material
       reveals Plath's predominant concern: "the nature of her being," which
       she sees as "a complex of irreconcilable antagonisms." This vision of
       herself explains the existence of both her "happy poems" and her
       suicide, which was not merely an escape, but "the only honorable
       exercise of her freedom." An analysis of *Three Women*, *Crossing the
       Water*, and *Winter Trees* is presented.

2   BEDFORD, JEAN. "Sylvia Plath and Suicide." *Digger* (November-
       December): 9.
           A review of A. Alvarez's *The Savage God*. Criticizes the
       author's naiveté in using his own suicide attempt as a way of explaining

8

suicide in general. Alvarez's view of Sylvia Plath is "sexist, romantically obtuse, and clouded by his partiality toward Ted Hughes."

3   DITSKY, JOHN. Review of *Winter Trees*. *Southern Humanities Review* 8 (Winter): 115-16.
  In this volume "Sylvia Plath is again as we have known her (again, as we have all wished to save her from being), the sorcerer's apprentice left barely in charge of her rebel materials."

4   DREXLER, ROSALYN. "Her Poetry, Not Her Death, Is Her Triumph." *New York Times, Biographical Edition* 5 (January): 106-7.
  Reprint of 1974.5.

5   _____. "Her Poetry, Not Her Death, Is Her Triumph." *New York Times*, 13 January, sec. 2, p. 3.
  Announces an upcoming evening of Sylvia Plath, which is to be brought to the Brooklyn Academy of Great Britain's Royal Shakespeare Company. Comments on the possibility that some of Plath's appeal may be due to her suicide. Attempts to show that any fascination with Plath should come from her work, not her death. That is, the work *deserves* to be the source of the fascination. Reprinted: 1974.4.

6   HAKEEM, A. "Sylvia Plath's 'Elm' and Munch's 'The Scream.'" *English Studies* 55 (December): 531-37.
  Points out the similarities between "expressionistic" painting and "confessional" poetry by comparing Plath's "Elm" to Munch's "The Scream." Each work represents a "personal angst, which finally leads to a scream of anguish." Ties both works to their "autobiographical antecedents." Judges Munch to be "far more imaginative" and a much better "craftsman" than Plath.

7   HARDWICK, ELIZABETH. "On Sylvia Plath." In *Seduction and Betrayal: Women and Literature*. New York: Random House, pp. 104-24.
  Reprint of 1971.B21*. Reprinted: 1973.11; 1985.10.

1974

8   HIMELICK, RAYMOND. "Notes on the Care and Feeding of Nightmares: Burton, Erasmus, and Sylvia Plath." *Western Humanities Review* 28 (Autumn): 313-26.

Discusses *The Bell Jar* by comparing and contrasting it with Burton's *Anatomy of Melancholy* and Erasmus' *Praise of Folly*. Plath's description of her own breakdown is, after all, nothing new. One notable contrast between Plath and Burton, however, is "in the handling of experience. . . . In *The Bell Jar* . . . [the emphasis] is always upon self. . . ." Burton's focus on the other hand, is "away from the Me and Now of the author. . . ." Concludes that the "older humanistic view of the human condition was both tougher-minded and less simplistic."

9   HOWE, IRVING. "Politics and Poetry." *Commentary* 58 (October): 9, 12.

Addresses an issue raised by an exchange of letters to the editor of *Commentary* published previously as responses to John Romano's article (see 1974.22). Plath's use of holocaust images in her poem "Daddy" is criticized.

10   HUGHES, CATHERINE. "Britain in Brooklyn – Royal Shakespearean Production from Sylvia Plath's Works." *America* 130 (9 February): 92.

Review of the stage production, *Sylvia Plath*, at the Brooklyn Academy of Music. Although the material is interesting and dramatic, "the production is . . . excessively histrionic, calling attention to itself." Such overkill is unnecessary because "Plath was her own melodrama, her own self-dramatization."

11   KALEM, T. E. "Toppled King/Torn Mind." *Time* 103 (28 January): 77.

A review of the stage performance of Plath's works by the Royal Shakespeare Repertory Theatre Group in Brooklyn. The performance is "rather grim for body and soul."

12   LIBBY, ANTHONY. "God's Lioness and the Priest of Sycorax: Plath and Hughes." *Contemporary Literature* 15 (Summer): 386-405.

1974

Discusses the ways in which Ted Hughes's and Sylvia Plath's poetic sensibilities and visions crossed over into each other's poetry. They exerted a "great stylistic and philosophical influence" on each other. "From the beginning they shared a vision of elemental conflict." Reprinted: 1984.22.

13   LINDBERG-SEYERSTED, BRITA. "Notes on Three Poems by Sylvia Plath." *Edda* 74: 47-54.

Disagrees with Ingrid Melander's opinion that in "Watercolour of Grantchester Meadows," Plath was being ironic in her description of the romantic, pastoral scene (see 1971. B39*). Plath was painting a picture of surface details only, "the way the black-gowned students . . . would see it, in their 'moony indolence of love.'" In reality such "peace and harmony" as the surface details seem to support do not in fact exist. Explains the last line of "Two Campers in Cloud Country" ("We'll wake blank-brained as water in the dawn.") as "purification." The excursion into the wilderness will wash the poem's speaker clean of the "banality" of the everyday. In "Daddy," Plath created a fictional model" of her father in order to carry out a ritual murder that would free her from the trauma of losing him. She made the model "monstrous" so that she would be able to go through with the murder and justify it afterward. There is no evidence, as some have suggested, that Otto Plath was in fact the hideous person represented in the poem.

14   McCLATCHY, J. D. "Staring from Her Hood of Bone: Adjusting to Sylvia Plath." In *American Poetry since 1960: Some Critical Perspectives*. Edited by Robert B. Shaw. Cheadle: Carcanet Press, pp. 155-66.

Establishes connections between the "transitional" poems in *Crossing the Water* and *Winter Trees* with those in *Ariel*. The latter volume, however, contains "an urgency and poignance that the earlier volumes lack." Plath consistently experiments with voice and reworks "the dilemma of the divided mind."

15   McKAY, D. F. "Aspects of Energy in the Poetry of Dylan Thomas and Sylvia Plath." *Critical Quarterly* 16 (Spring): 53-67.

Begins with a discussion of Ezra Pound's definition of "great literature" as "language charged with meaning to the utmost possible degree." This definition is applied to the work of both Plath and Thomas through an analysis of several poems. Concludes that "[i]n general, ... Plath's poetic experience takes in the extremes, invoking the absent afflatus and transmitting the potency of a dominating animus, while Thomas variously resists and allies himself with a primal force."

16   NORTHOUSE, CAMERON, and WALSH, THOMAS P. *Sylvia Plath and Anne Sexton: A Reference Guide*. Boston: G. K. Hall & Co., 143 pp.
       An annotated bibliography of criticism on Sylvia Plath and Anne Sexton. Material on Plath covers 1960-1973.

17   OATES, JOYCE CAROL. "The Death Throes of Romanticism: The Poetry of Sylvia Plath." In *Contemporary Poetry in America: Essays and Interviews*. Edited by Robert Boyers. New York: Schocken, pp. 139-56.
       Reprint of 1973.B11*. Reprinted: 1974.18; 1977.34; 1985.19.

18   ____. "The Death Throes of Romanticism: The Poetry of Sylvia Plath." In *New Heaven, New Earth*. New York: Vanguard, pp. 113-40.
       Reprint of 1973.B11*. Reprinted: 1974.17; 1977.34; 1985.19.

19   OLIVER, EDITH. "Off Broadway." *New Yorker* 49 (28 January): 69.
       Review of "Sylvia Plath," a "dramatized setting of her writings." The words are taken from *The Bell Jar*, several poems, and "Three Women." Plath's words are "so well spoken that the poet herself is all but present."

20   ORGEL, SHELLEY. "Sylvia Plath: Fusion with the Victim and Suicide." *Psychoanalytic Quarterly* 43 (Fall): 262-87.
       Discusses the psychological ramifications of Plath's tendency toward "the simultaneous identification with the torturer and victim." Maintains that "the interrelationships between identification with the chronically ill, the dead oedipal father, and the more primitive identification with the pre-oedipal mother (parent) need to be

considered." Analyzes several of Plath's poems and parts of *The Bell Jar*. What caused Plath's death was her "ability to feel for, to become one with, all men and women, all animate and inanimate objects, both as aggressor and victim." Reprinted: 1981.16 under a slightly different title.

21 "Plathiana." *New York Times Book Review*, 15 December, p. 29.
    Reports on the publication and editing process of *Letters Home*. Editor Frances McCullough is quoted as saying "the letters have 'a fantastic sense of immediacy as if you'd just ripped open the envelope.'"

22 ROMANO, JOHN. "Sylvia Plath Reconsidered." *Commentary* 57 (April): 47-52.
    Claims that those critics, like A. Alvarez, who view Sylvia Plath as "a martyr ... to the demands of her art" do the poet a great disservice, however good their intentions may be. They take part in a "death-happy exultation." The poems themselves lend credence to this interpretation only when the reader fails to separate the poetic "I" from the poet herself. It is the *persona* of the poems who presents suicide and suicide attempts as "performances," not Plath. *The Bell Jar* is discussed and compared to Salinger's *The Catcher in the Rye*.

23 STAINTON, RITA T. "Vision and Voice in Three Poems by Sylvia Plath." *Windless Orchard* 17 (Spring): 31-36.
    Traces the permutations of Plath's "haunted vision" from her earliest through her last work. The terror always existed, but was somewhat obscured in the early work by the poet's "concerns for form, control and obliquity." In her later poems, however, she stood face to face with the "disquieting muses" that were her "'traveling companions.'"

24 TAYLOR, ANDREW. "Sylvia Plath's Mirror and Beehive." *Meanjin Quarterly* 339 (September): 256-65.
    Takes issue with those critics who maintain that the issue most central to Plath's work was her "self destructiveness." The struggle between the two sides of her self is represented by "images of silver and whiteness" on the one hand, and by "colour and darkness," earth,

1974

natural things on the other. The poet's suicide "in no way alters the statements she made in her poems."

25   UROFF, MARGARET D. "Sylvia Plath's Women." *Concerning Poetry* 7 (Spring): 45-56.
      Explores the women in Plath's poetry as "literary figures" rather than as versions of the poet herself, a view that much previous criticism has taken. Examines the poetry in chronological order and finds that the female personae represent the "higher order" of existence, intellectual and pure. The men, on the other hand, are "brutish and physical," often even being transformed into "predators."

26   VENDLER, HELEN. "La Poesia de Sylvia Plath." *Plural* 33 (15 June): 6-14.
      Spanish translation by Ulalume Gonzalez de Leon of A1971.54. See Appendix.

27   ZATLIN, LINDA G. "'This holocaust I walk in': The Poetic Vision of Sylvia Plath." *University of Michigan Papers in Women's Studies* 1 (October): 158-73.
      Presents a thematic analysis of Plath's alternatives to death – optimism, then disillusion. Dates the poems by year of publication rather than by year of composition. There are "two parallel streams" in her work: "the desire for identity and the desire for death." Her life was not "a linear movement to suicide." Instead, it was made up of "two contradictory and tortuous streams controlling her vision." The confrontation with death was only "one part of her larger response to the psyche-crushing problems posed by existence in the 20th century."

1975

1   BALITAS, VINCENT D. "A Note on Sylvia Plath's 'The Hanging Man.'" *Notes and Queries*, n.s. 22 (May): 208.
      Suggests that one possible source of Plath's poem could be a woodcut titled "The Hanging Man" by Leonard Baskin, an American artist Plath greatly admired.

14

2 _____. "On Becoming a Witch: A Reading of Sylvia Plath's 'Witch Burning.'" *Studies in the Humanities* 4 (February): 27-30.

    Analyzes "Witch Burning" as one of Plath's many poems which derive "intensity from the presentation of altering states and/or degrees of consciousness." In this particular poem, the persona actually becomes a witch and concludes that the result of the transformation is positive. The process of becoming a witch is the only painful part.

3 CARAHER, BRIAN. "The Problematic of Body and Language in Sylvia Plath's 'Tulips.'" *Paunch* 42-43 (December): 76-89.

    Discusses the various kinds of "tension" within Plath's "Tulips." Those tensions are created in three ways: 1) There is empathy but no actual identification with the emotional state of the persona, 2) the disparity between the persona's "assumptions and values" and those of others (readers), and 3) "the tension between speaker and the language and structure of her speaking." The resolution in the poem is that bodily existence is a workable value in the face of civilization's misvaluations.

4 CRAIN, JANE LARKIN. Review of *Letters Home*. *Saturday Review*, n.s. 3 (15 November): 26.

    Characterizes the Plath who penned the letters as bearing nearly no resemblance to the Plath of *Ariel*. The collection will "irritate" those who have tired of "the Plath mystique."

5 CUNNINGHAM, STUART. "Bibliography: Sylvia Plath." *Hecate* 1 (July): 95-112.

    Provides a list of both primary and secondary Plath sources. Includes "a list recording the individual publication of each piece of poetry, prose, and drama in journals and anthologies."

6 DAVIS, ROBIN REED. "'Now I Have Lost Myself': A Reading of Sylvia Plath's 'Tulips.'" *Paunch* 42-43 (December): 97-104.

    Begins by noting the many typing errors in *Ariel*. No real study of Plath's development as a poet can be made until "a well-edited collected edition is published." Goes on to give an analysis of "Tulips." The poetic persona comes to the realization that "the real source of

1975

[her] problem ... is not external, the tulips, but internal, in her own heart." She becomes aware of the love she feels "for the very self she has striven ... to annihilate."

7   DUFFY, MARTHA. "Two Lives." *Time* 106 (24 November): 101-2.
       Letters Home presents a different view of Sylvia Plath than does *The Bell Jar*. Gives an overview of the content of the letters and speculates on the reasons Aurelia Plath chose to publish them. Reprinted: 1988.20.

8   EFRON, ARTHUR. "Plath's 'Tulips': A Festival." *Paunch* 42-43 (December): 65.
       Observes in this introduction to several essays on the poem that "Tulips" is often neglected in much Plath criticism, apparently because it does not "fit the critical image of Plath."

9   ____. "Sylvia Plath's 'Tulips' and Literary Criticism." *Paunch* 42-43 (December): 69-75.
       Contends that what is "problematical" about the poem is that the final stanza contains both "ambivalence" and "resolutions." The only readers who will be unable to experience the poem fully are those who absolutely reject two notions: 1) "that an ambivalent self-acceptance can be genuine, and a real resolution," and 2) "that ... biological existence provides the only reliable mode of self-acceptance."

10   ____. "'Tulips': Text and Assumptions." *Paunch* 42-43 (December): 110-22.
       Presents a detailed explication of the last stanza of "Tulips" as part of a classroom discussion of the poem. One of the few points of argument among students was that the stanza is "a resolution in which the speaker begins to move toward health." Discusses other critics' (Uroff, Davis, Perloff) responses to the poem.

11   GUSTAFSON, RICHARD. "'Time Is a Waiting Woman': New Poetic Icons." *Midwest Quarterly* 16 (Spring): 318-27.

1975

Briefly discusses Plath's "Daddy" as an example of how women poets are turning "to the paternal. . . [in] a search for a cultural stability to offer their personae an individual identity." However, the male "father-lover-husband" is seen as failing in all three roles: "He cannot be God because the century has been so much hell; he cannot be father because fatherhood has brought forth living pain and no consolation; he cannot be lover and husband because his touch is violent."

12   HOWARD, MAUREEN. "The Girl Who Tried to Be Good." *New York Times Book Review*, 14 December, pp. 1-2.
        Review essay on *Letters Home*. Because Plath was determinedly happy and optimistic in these letters to her mother, this volume is more like fiction than truth.

13   HOWE, IRVING. "The Plath Celebration: A Partial Dissent." In *Poetry Dimension Annual 3: The Best of the Poetry Year*. Edited by Dannie Abse. New York: St. Martin's Press, pp. 43-57.
        Reprint of 1972.B12*,"Sylvia Plath: A Partial Disagreement." Reprint of 1973.15. Reprinted: 1977.24.

14   JEFFERSON, MARGO. "Who Was Sylvia?" *Newsweek* 86 (22 December): 83.
        Review of *Letters Home*. Plath cannot be judged by these letters because they are nearly all written to a single person, her mother. Thus, she presented only "that facet of [her]self [she felt would] be most appreciated." In addition, the letters are too heavily edited to present an accurate portrait.

15   JONG, ERICA. "Letters Focus Exquisite Rage of Sylvia Plath." *Los Angeles Times Book Review*, 23 November, pp. 1, 10.
        Recommends *Letters Home* as essential for a better understanding of Plath and her work. It "adds another voice to [those] of Sylvia Plath we already know." Unfortunately, it is more interesting "for what it excludes [than] for what it includes," having been "edited and pruned" by Plath's mother, Aurelia Schober Plath and her husband Ted Hughes. Reprinted: 1988.39.

17

1975

16 LANE, GARY MARTIN. "Sylvia Plath's 'The Hanging Man': A Further Note." *Contemporary Poetry* 2 (Spring): 40-43.
　　Responds to G. S. Fraser's earlier discussion of "The Hanging Man" (see 1973.9). The key to understanding the poem is knowledge of Plath's biography. The event which "urged [the poem's] making" was the electroconvulsive therapy Plath received when she was twenty and the ultimate failure of this treatment – a failure of which at some level of consciousness Plath was aware.

17 LEHMANN-HAUPT, CHRISTOPHER. "From Outside the Bell Jar." *New York Times*, 9 December, p. 39.
　　Characterizes *Letters Home* as a "puzzling book," one which "serves to dispel" the Plath myth – that the poet "offer[ed] herself up for the sake of her art." The letters portray Plath as an entirely different person from the one presented in *The Bell Jar*. Given her other work and her suicide, the letters create a "sense of unreality."

18 MOLLINGER, ROBERT. "A Symbolic Complex: Images of Death and Daddy in the Poetry of Sylvia Plath." *Descant* 19 (Winter): 44-52.
　　Observes that Plath's symbols of death – "the sea; the color black, and the associated grey and shadow; coldness, in the form of ice and snow; stone, and the related image of marble; the machine or engine . . . ; and serpents and snakes" – are always somehow associated with the father. "Behind any image of death lies the father; where death is, there also is the father." This contention is supported by a close reading of several poems.

19 ___. "Sylvia Plath's 'Private Ground.'" *Notes on Contemporary Literature* 5 (March): 14-15.
　　Explores Plath's "Private Ground" (from *Crossing the Water*) as a poem which can be read from two perspectives. "From one . . . the poem seems to be about the "preservation of life . . . [F]rom another, . . . it appears to be about the speaker's own death."

20 MORRIS, IRENE V. "Sylvia Plath at Newnham, A Tutorial Recollection." *Newnham College Roll: Letter* (January): 45-47.

1975

Impressions of Sylvia Plath by one of her tutors at Newnham College, Cambridge. Remembers Plath as "youthfully and touchingly enthusiastic . . . even somewhat naive and over-emotional." Reprinted: 1988.57.

21   NOBLE, DONALD. "Letters of Sylvia Plath." *Boston Sunday Herald Advertiser*, 28 December, section 3, p. 62.

Summarizes the major autobiographical events outlined in *Letters Home*. Plath's mother edited the book because she felt it was time Plath's readers knew the forces which shaped her life, her work, and her death.

22   OUELLET, NORMA. "*Letters Home* Provides Rare Glimpse of Sylvia Plath." *Townsman* (Wellesley, Mass.), 20 November, pp. 1, 8.

Quotes Aurelia Plath, who says the reason she published her daughter's letters was that "the image projected by . . . *The Bell Jar* was not Sylvia." Compiling the letters was a difficult task partly because Sylvia did not date them. Mrs. Plath criticizes readers of *The Bell Jar* for assuming that Esther's mother is based entirely on Sylvia's own mother, maintaining that Sylvia merely "had the fine gift for manipulating and fusing the experiences in her life to fit her creative endeavors."

23   PADNOS, PEG. "Sylvia Plath's Letters Serve as Unpremeditated Autobiography." *Chicago Tribune*, 30 November, section 7, p. 3.

Review of *Letters Home*. Because they are spontaneous, these letters are "more satisfying" than Plath's "self-conscious first novel," *The Bell Jar*. They combine "the immediacy of diary and the dispassion of biography."

24   "Plath." *New York Times Book Review*, 14 December, p. 37.

Discusses the publication process of *Letters Home*. Although Aurelia Plath possessed the letters, Ted Hughes owns the literary rights to them. He granted Mrs. Plath the copyright but reserved the right to final approval. When Hughes received the letters the second time, he decided there were too many references "to living people" and made deletions in the manuscript. The publisher's lawyers later restored

1975

those deletions that "presented no libel or invasion of privacy problems."

25   Review of *Letters Home. Booklist* 72 (15 October): 272-73.
        The letters shed little light on Plath's craft as a writer but will be "required reading" for students of Plath.

26   Review of *Letters Home. Kirkus Reviews* 43 (15 September): 1103-4.
        Questions the value of the letters "as autobiography, as amplification, or as anything except externalization of details." The tone is often effusive enough to be embarrassing.

27   Review of *Letters Home. New Yorker* 51 (22 December): 95-96.
        The letters are so full of joy and "zest" for life that the reader is tempted to believe that Plath's was "a tragic death but not, perhaps, a tragic life."

28   Review of *Letters Home. Publishers Weekly* 208 (18 August): 58.
        The letters provide important source materials "for future studies of this extraordinary poet."

29   ROSENSTEIN, HARRIET. "'To the Most Wonderful Mummy a Girl Ever Had.'" *Ms.* 4 (December): 45-49.
        The "Sivvy" of *Letters Home* is "all ardor, gush, and earnestness," bearing no resemblance at all to the *Ariel* poet. The book's major interest lies in the "contradictions" it presents "between the poet we know and the daughter we discover here." Concludes by offering one possible truth the letters tell: "Plath attempted to be to her husband what her mother had been to her – cheerleader, typist, agent, protector, slavey, and spiritual twin."

30   SMITH, STAN. "Attitudes Counterfeiting Life: The Irony of Artifice in Sylvia Plath's *The Bell Jar*." *Critical Quarterly* 17 (Autumn): 247-60.
        Argues that "the main principle [of the novel is] a series of contrasts and analogies between 'personal experience' and a variety of

forms of 'artifice.'" Just as "the younger Esther" scrutinizes and constantly re-examines her life experiences, so "Esther the narrator"
becomes the audience to her own past, detached and objective. "Plath
the actual author manipulat[es] a continuous and ironic parallel but the
condition of schizophrenic self-alienation and the familiar devises of
narrative technique."

31 SPENDAL, R. J. "Sylvia Plath's 'Cut.'" *Modern Poetry Studies* 6
    (Autumn): 128-34.
        Contends that in Plath's "Cut," as in several of her other
poems, the poet "turns familiar bodily ills into metaphors of psychic
affliction." Praises the poem as a superbly crafted piece and presents a
close structural, linguistic analysis of it.

32 STONE, CAROL. "Three Mother-Daughter Poems: The Struggle
    for Separation." *Contemporary Psychoanalysis* 11 (April): 227-39.
        Begins from the premise that poetry is useful for "psychological
insight" especially that insight gained by studying "the girl's relationship"
to both the father and the mother. Analyzes the work of Anne Sexton,
Erica Jong, and Sylvia Plath. Plath's "The Disquieting Muses" is
discussed as a poem in which the persona gains "autonomy . . . through
withdrawal from the mother who fails her daughter on the most basic
level."

33 TYLER, RALPH. "High-Wire Act." *Bookletter* 2 (December): 1, 16.
        Review of *Letters Home*. Summarizes the author's interviews
with Plath in early 1960. The letters themselves are "important social
documents of the 1950s," but may not provide a complete picture of
Plath. By the time the readers finish, they will be so "involved" with her
that they will want to know what went wrong with her marriage.
Unfortunately, those letters are missing.

34 UROFF, M. D. "Sylvia Plath's 'Tulips.'" *Paunch* 42-43 (December):
    90-96.
        Argues that "Tulips" is a poem about being anesthetized and
subsequently regaining both consciousness and pain. Symbolically, it is
also about "becoming somebody after having been reduced to nobody."

1975

The peacefulness that comes from being nobody is not worth the price and must be rejected. When, at the end of the poem, she connects the tulips to her "wound" she is "beginning to exercise the creative associative, imaginative activity of the healthy heart."

35   YOSHIDA, SACHIKO. "Incense of Death: Sylvia Plath no Sonzai no Kaku." *Eigo Seinen* 120 (1 January): 488-89.
      Begins with a discussion of "The Manor Garden," in which all the images represent death. Traces the connections between this poem's themes and those of "Lady Lazarus," "The Munich Mannequins," and "The Moon and the Yew Tree." It is not an exaggeration to say that all Plath's poetry is death-obsessed. In Japanese.

36   ZAIDMAN, LAURA M. Review of *Letters Home*. *Library Journal* 100 (15 October): 1916.
      The letters offer a hitherto unknown "dimension of Plath's complex persona." The insights offered by Mrs. Plath are uneven in their value.

37   ZIVLEY, SHERRY LUTZ. "Sylvia Plath's Beekeeping Poems." *Poet and Critic* 9: 32-39.
      Analyzes each of Plath's six beekeeping poems as expressions of "a woman's urgent need to be free from the coercions of men, children, and society." Her imagery and symbolism are ambiguous, shifting among and even within poems. She "identified her speaker alternately or simultaneously with ignorant observer, beekeeper, worker bee, or queen."

1976

1   ACKROYD, PETER. "Dear Mummy, I Hate You." *Spectator*, 24
     April, p. 21.
          Reviews *Letters Home*. The letters reveal much about Plath's
     art but little about her life.

2   ADAMS, PHOEBE-LOU. Review of *Letters Home*. *Atlantic Month-
     ly* 237 (February): 11.
          Finds Mrs. Plath's editing a disservice to readers. Her deleting
     of all her daughter's negative comments "has resulted in a gush of
     girlish glee that is unbelievable and even revolting." Those who have
     read the *Ariel* poems will be unable to accept this portrait of the artist.

3   ALLEN, MARY. "Sylvia Plath's Defiance: *The Bell Jar*." In *The
     Necessary Blankness: Women in Major American Fiction of the
     Sixties*. Urbana: University of Illinois Press, pp. 160-78.
          Traces Esther Greenwood's systematic rejection of the
     traditional woman's role she was expected to assume. She refuses
     preoccupation with beauty, "passion for popularity," "romantic notions
     about sexual experience or men," and conventional attitudes toward
     marriage, motherhood, and babies. Unfortunately, "her brilliance and
     accomplishments have no power to lead her to a place in the world."
     Women who refuse conventional roles have no other role to choose.

4   ALVAREZ, A. "Inside the Bell Jar." *Observer* 18 April, p. 23.
          Review of *Letters Home*. They show the stable, positive side of
     Plath's personality, partly because of Aurelia Plath's heavy editing, but
     also because there was actually such a side to Sylvia's personality. The
     only "taboo" subject in the letters seems to be her father, Otto Plath,
     who is mentioned only once in the 500 pages of letters.

5   AXELROD, STEVEN GOULD. "Plath's and Lowell's Last Words."
     Pacific Coast Philology 11 (October): 5-14.
          Views both Plath and Lowell as "internaliz[ing] the moral and
     political disturbances of our times, and undergo[ing] them personally."
     Confessional poetry such as theirs overturns the "impersonality and
     autonomy of Modernism" and returns us to the personal poem made

public. Plath's last poems evince a "failure of ideas." Even her best work is rooted in "malignity."

6   BALLIF, GENE. "Facing the Worst: A View from Minerva's Buckler." *Parnassus: Poetry in Review* 5 (Fall/Winter): 231-59.
        Establishes correspondences between Plath's letters to her mother and several of her poems. Thus, the article emphasizes the importance of biography to Plath's work. However, the author professes agreement with "M. L. Rosenthal's reminder that 'a poem is an aesthetic projection of the psychological motive behind it, perhaps, but it is not the same thing as those motives.'" Still, "a poem . . . has to be read for what it is on the surface before it can take root in imaginations that sense in it something else."

7   BLOW, SIMON. "Rendezvous with Death." *Books and Bookmen* 21 (July): 44, 46.
        Review essay on *Letters Home*. The personality of the author of these letters is at odds with that of the author of *The Bell Jar* and *Ariel*. The development of these dual personalities has its roots in the experience of Plath's father's death. Includes a brief biography.

8   BRANS, JO. "'The Girl Who Wanted to Be God.'" *Southwest Review* 61 (Summer): 325-8.
        The letters in *Letters Home* reveal little "of the Sylvia of the poetry." Because of the "discrepancy between [the personalities of] the poetry and letters," and because the letters are "selected" and edited, their reliability is negligible. Reprinted: 1984.4; 1988.11.

9   BROE, MARY LYNN. Review of *Letters Home. Journal of Modern Literature* 5: 787-89.
        The major disadvantage of the letters is that they "may obscure the more muted details important to the future of Plath scholarship." Their major contribution is their "nuts-and-bolts commentary on [Plath's] developing talent."

1976

10 BUELL, FREDERICK. "Sylvia Plath's Traditionalism." *Boundary 2* 5 (Fall): 195-211.
    The Bell Jar and *Letters Home* place Plath within the post-Romantic and symbolist literary tradition. "One can see in Plath many echoes of the Prufrock self-consciousness." Reprinted: 1984.6

11 BUTSCHER, EDWARD. *Sylvia Plath: Method and Madness*. New York: Seabury Press, 388 pp.
    First full biography of Plath.

12 BYATT, A. S. "Mirror, Mirror on the Wall." *New Statesman* 91 (23 April): 541-42.
    Comments on the similarities and differences between the Plath who wrote *Ariel* and the one who wrote letters to her mother. Uses "The Disquieting Muses" as "a clue to the relationship" between these two selves. All the letters are "strenuously cheery," possibly because they have been extensively edited.

13 COHEN, ED. "Seeking the One True Plath." *Chicago Reader*, 5 November, p. 22.
    Argues that Plath would be "horrified, astonished, and bemused" could she know the countless misconceptions and misinterpretations about her work that have been published in the name of scholarship since her death. Members of Plath's "mythic circle" have so distorted and obscured Plath and her work that the "public may never get a glimpse of the real Sylvia again." Foremost among the offenders is A. Alvarez, who is called "a consummate literary whore."

14 COSGRAVE, MARY SILVA. Review of *Letters Home*. *Horn Book Magazine* 52 (April): 185.
    Discusses the variations of tone in the letters, which ranges from "ecstatic" to "strained and exhausted." The letters reveal "an intense, mercurial, sensitive, self-indulgent, gifted young person who lived exuberantly and died tragically."

1976

15 CROOME, LESLEY. "Pictures of the Mind." *Times Literary Supplement*, 2 April, p. 396.
Review of *The Bed Book*. The poetry here is considerably less intense than the author's "adult poetry." The verses "make up for what they lack in polish by the disarmingly casual air with which they appear to have been penned."

16 CURTIS, CATHY. "In Her Letters, She Wanted to Be a Cosmo Girl." *Daily Californian*, 6 February, pp. 15,17.
Review of *Letters Home*. This volume will disappoint readers looking for evidence of a deprived tragic childhood. The letters are chatty and "bubbly." The writer presents herself as having "tried to live in an unreal world in which everything is done as it 'should be' – from the right dress to the right attitude towards one's husband."

17 DABYDEEN, CYRIL. Review of *Letters Home*. *Dalhousie Review* 56 (Spring): 166-67.
Letters Home will help correct the widespread notion that Plath had a "negative relationship with her mother." The letters show Plath's intense desire both to write brilliantly and "to enjoy, 'a charmed plathian existence.'"

18 De LAURETIS, TERESA. "Rebirth in *The Bell Jar*." *Women's Studies* 3:173-83.
A psychological study which advances the idea that *The Bell Jar* is a successful "novel of the self much in the sense in which Joyce's, Kafka's, Proust's, and Svevo's are." *The Bell Jar* is an account of Esther's disintegration and subsequent rebirth and thus "is built on the mythical descent-ascent pattern." Maintains that the first two chapters introduce "all the major themes and motifs of the novel." Briefly compares *The Bell Jar* to *Autobiography of a Schizophrenic Girl*. Reprinted: 1988.19.

19 DESOUZA, EUNICE. "Humanizing the Myth." *Times of India*, 18 July, p. 10.
Review of *Letters Home*. Suggests that Plath's mother published her daughter's letters in an effort to "justify herself" after the

'distortions' of *The Bell Jar*. While the "sunny and exuberant" Sylvia is certainly present in the letters, "the potential suicide is there too."

20   DILL, BARBARA. "Picturely Books for Children." *Wilson Library Bulletin* 51 (October): 132.
       Review of *The Bed Book*. Wonderfully imaginative, the book could be used "as a jumping off point for ... children's art work or writing."

21   DINNAGE, ROSEMARY. "A Girl from Wellesley." *Times Literary Supplement*, 23 April, p. 480.
       Review of *Letters Home*. Presents readers with the difficult task of reconciling the writer of these letters, full of "girlish gush," with the poet of *Ariel*.

22   EDER, DORIS. "Portrait of the Artist as a Young Woman." *Book Forum* 2 (Spring): 242-54.
       Review of *Letters Home*. The letters are "Aurelia Plath's self-vindication as a mother." They present Sylvia Plath as optimistic, intelligent, loving daughter, not as tortured, death-obsessed poet. Reading this volume is painful because it reveals the extent of Plath's dependency on her mother. "Sylvia felt she had to justify her mother's existence as well as her own."

23   ERIKSSON, P. D. "Sylvia Plath" *Unisa English Studies* 14 (September): 95-97.
       Review of *Letters Home*. Emphasizes the extreme difference between the person who wrote the letters and the one who wrote the poetry. The latter is barely perceptible here.

24   H., M. R. Review of *The Bed Book*. *Junior Bookshelf* 40 (June): 167.
       Describes the book as "entirely charming." It does not warrant "publication alone as an entire book," however.

1976

25 HARTHILL, ROSEMARY. "From Sivvy, with Love." *Times Educational Supplement*, 14 May, p. 20.

Review of *Letters Home*. They reveal the writer's obsessive need for "other people's praise and terms of success." One reason for her "tragedy" was the "conflict between what she wanted or thought herself to be and what she was."

26 HAUGHTON, HUGH. "In Her Mother's Kingdom." *Times Higher Education Supplement*, 16 July, p. 15.

Review of *Letters Home*. The letters are so banal and mundane that they "do not help the readers of her poetry" at all. The poetry and *The Bell Jar* tell us far more about Plath than these letters do.

27 H[EARNE], B[ETSY]. Review of *The Bed Book*. *Booklist* 73 (1 September): 41-42.

The poem is "inventive," stretching young imaginations just far enough. It "reads aloud like a dream."

28 HOLBROOK, DAVID. *Sylvia Plath: Poetry and Existence*. London: Athlone Press, 308 pp.

Approaches Plath phenomenologically. The thesis of the book is stated at the end of the first chapter: " . . . [Plath's] predicament was terrible: but even more terrible was the way in which our society applauded her for the falsification, while remaining deaf to her truth."

29 HUGHES, OLWYN. Letter to the editor. *New York Review of Books*, 30 September, pp. 42-43.

Takes issue with a previously published review of Edward Butscher's biography of Plath, *Sylvia Plath: Method and Madness* (see 1976.11). Maintains that this biography is not "worthy of critical attention." Instead, it is merely a "rubbishy hotch-potch."

30 JUHASZ, SUZANNE. "'The Blood Jet': The Poetry of Sylvia Plath." In *Naked and Fiery Forms: Modern American Poetry by Women, a New Tradition*. New York and London: Harper and Row; New York: Octagon Books, pp. 85-116.

Offers a reading of Plath's poetry which rejects those appraisals of her work which "[allow] her to be appreciated and even venerated as a wonderfully sensitive soul who transcended life by death and art; a myth; a prophetess." At the opposite extreme, it also rejects the "anticult, purely literary approach." Plath personae must be approached on a plane somewhere in between these two extremes. Her poetic voice is "a projection," not her actual human voice; nevertheless, she herself and "the experience of which she writes" are actually in the poems. Reprinted: 1978.9.

31 KARLIN, BARBARA. Review of *The Bed Book*. *New York Times Book Review*, 14 November, p. 38.
     This children's verse suffers from an excess of "cuteness," making the book a disappointment.

32 KENNER, HUGH. "Sweet Seventeen." *National Review* 18 (30 April): 459-60.
     Review of *Letters Home*. What is surprising about this volume is to learn that Plath, a gifted Smith College student, was "pouring out *Seventeen* [Magazine] idiom."

33 KINZIE, MARY. "A New Life and Other Plath Controversies." *American Poetry Review* 5 (March-April): 5-8.
     Review of *Letters Home*. Compares the account of Plath's life given in the letters with that given in Edward Butscher's biography of Plath. (See 1976.11.)

34 KROLL, JUDITH. *Chapters in a Mythology: The Poetry of Sylvia Plath*. New York: Harper and Row, 303 pp.
     Examines Plath's work "on its own terms which is to say, as literature." Plath's suicide is irrelevant, even though many critics have "been entangled in a fascination with [it]." While Plath is generally considered a "confessional" poet, her poems go far beyond the personal and the everyday. They "are transmuted into something impersonal by being absorbed into a timeless mythic system, [which] has its basis in her biography, but . . . becomes more symbolic and archetypal."

1976

The "motifs" of Plath's myth are 1) the male as both god and devil, 2) the false and true selves, and 3) death and rebirth.

If Plath had lived, she would likely have claimed more "of what Ted Hughes calls her free and controlled access to depths formerly reserved to the primitive ecstatic priests, shamans, and holy men.'"

35 KROOK, DOROTHEA. "Recollections of Sylvia Plath." *Critical Quarterly* 18 (Winter): 5-14.

The author, one of Plath's teachers at Cambridge, recalls her academic relationship with Plath. Conjectures that Plath's extreme "academic effort" was actually a "struggle for 'normalcy' against the forces of disintegration within her." Reprinted: 1977.29.

36 LEWIS, MARJORIE. Review of *The Bed Book*. *School Library Journal* 23 (September): 104.

The verse is unimaginative and boring enough to "put anyone to sleep." It disappoints readers who rightfully expect much more from a creative genius like Plath.

37 McCULLOUGH, FRANCES. "Advice and Consent." *Atlantic Monthly* 237 (May): 31.

A letter to the editor concerning *Letters Home*. McCullough maintains that Aurelia Plath never suggested the letters be edited for the purpose of covering up painful truths.

38 McLELLAN, JOSEPH. "What Ever Happened to Mother Goose?" *Washington Post*, 7 November, "Book World" section, pp. 5-6.

Review of *The Bed Book*. It stands in the "mainstream of traditional children's literature." Children will find the poem charming and delightful.

39 MALOFF, SAUL. "The Poet as Cult Goddess." *Commonweal* 103 (June): 371-4.

Judges *The Bell Jar* as narratively "flat" and void of imagination. The events are strictly autobiography, "untransfigured" and without illumination. Suggests that Plath used the novel to say all the nasty things she omitted in her letters. Attributes Plath's fame to the fact that she committed suicide, not to her genius as a poet. Her work is not of sufficient importance to justify a serious study of either it or its author.

40   MAY, DERWENT. "Panicky Pictures." *Listener* 96 (11 November): 626-27.
        Review of *The Bed Book*. Provides "innocent pleasure" in an "absolutely delightful poem."

41   MEEK, MARGARET. Review of *The Bed Book*. *School Librarian* 24 (June): 138.
        Brings "both poetry and pleasure" to the reader. Praises Quentin Blake's illustrations.

42   MILLER, KARL. "Sylvia Plath's Apotheosis." *New York Review of Books* 23 (24 June): 3-8.
        Review of *Letters Home*. Comments on their "insufficiency." The letters say little about what many scholars regard as the central event in Plath's life – the death of her father. "Aurelia Plath does not disguise her concern to sugar her daughter's strange history." These letters do exactly that, and nothing else.

43   MOONEY, BEL. "Extravagant Heart." *Guardian*, 22 April, p. 9.
        A review of *Letters Home*. The letters will disappoint Plath's "hysterical female acolytes" because their tone is nearly unreservedly joyful and healthy. The personality they express is the opposite of the one expressed in Plath's poetry.

44   NEVILLE, JILL. "The Sylvia Plath Industry." *Sydney Morning Herald*, 3 April, p. 18.
        A review essay of *Letters Home*. The letters were not written out of duty. The later ones were sometimes used as a kind of "medicine" to help pull Plath out of her depression. They prove that Plath had "promoted" her poetry all her life. "[T]he inner truth of Sylvia Plath and her genius is contained in her poetry – but for those who are interested

1976

in the human being, ... these letters will have a poignant and compelling power."

45 PERLOFF, MARJORIE. "Breaking the Bell Jar." *Washington Post*, 4 April, pp. H1-H2.
    Comments on Plath's "fragmented" self. She was obsessed with pleasing others, – "the famous, the established, the arbiters of taste" – not herself, through her successes at publishing. Edward Butscher's biography of Plath finally "explodes ... A. Alvarez's romantic myth ... of Sylvia Plath as ... the poet who died."

46 PLATH, AURELIA SCHOBER, and ROBINSON, ROBERT. "Sylvia Plath's *Letters Home*: Some Reflections by Her Mother." *Listener* 95 (22 April): 515-16.
    An interview with Mrs. Plath. Emphasizes Plath's ability to manipulate experience and fuse characters as "part of the creative act." The characters in her fiction and the personae in her poems are not biographical representations of real people in her life.

47 RABAN, JONATHON. "Through the Looking-Glass." *Sunday Times*, 25 April, p. 41.
    Review of *Letters Home*. Exposes Plath's driving ambition to be the best and brightest "person on earth." Readers will be left with the sense that Plath's literary work was merely "the surplus left over from the even more ... demanding art of facing her mother." The number of letters itself suggests "something obsessional in the relationship." The persona presented here is "a mask" that thinly disguises the rage beneath it.

48 RATCLIFFE, MICHAEL. "Miss America and the Lorelei." *Times*, 19 April, p. 5.
    Review of *Letters Home*. Offers a brief biography of both Plath's parents. Plath's temperament was "informed with ... German qualities and aspirations." The picture of life Plath paints here is idyllic. The book is "astonishing, occasionally trivial," but never boring.

49   REED, NANCY GAIL. "Still Those Ellipses. . . ." *Christian Science Monitor*, 7 January, p. 23.
      Review of *Letters Home*. Maintains that the letters portray Plath as "very human" and approachable despite her "almost mind-boggling talent."

50   Review of *The Bed Book*. *Publishers Weekly* 209 (21 June): 92.
      Written for her own children, this book proves that Plath "had her merry moments." Its popularity is certain to be long-lived.

51   Review of *Letters Home*. *Choice* 13 (May): 371.
      The main value of the letters is that they present "quite a different view of [Plath's] relationship with her mother from that recorded in *The Bell Jar*.

52   Review of *Letters Home*. *Economist* 259 (1 May): 124.
      Calls Plath a "compulsive letter-writer" whose personality as displayed in these letters is very different from the one seen in *The Bell Jar*. They are valuable only as a "mother's memorial to a loved and mostly loving daughter."

53   ROLAND, LAURIN K. "Sylvia Plath's 'Lesbos': A Self Divided." *Concerning Poetry* 9 (Fall): 61-65.
      Contends that "Lesbos" contains not a dialogue between two women but a "dramatic monologue" between separate halves of a divided self. Because it treats a serious subject "in a light, . . . even frivolous manner," the poem may "be viewed as a burlesque in the literary sense of the word."

54   ROSENSTEIN, HARRIET. "Pure Gold Baby." *New Review* 3 (May): 53-57.
      Review of *Letters Home*. The letters' major effect is their revelation of the "contradiction between the poet we know and the daughter we discover here." Aurelia Plath's preface is also disconcerting because it "dissociates [Plath's] writings, her self-destruction and even portions of her correspondence from the rising biographical action

1976

through which she . . . directs us." Few of the personalities projected in the letters "ring true." Provides a somewhat psychological analysis of the mother-daughter relationship revealed throughout the letters.

55   RUBENSTEIN, ROBERTA. "Virginia Woolf and Sylvia Plath: Inner Truths." *Progressive* 40 (March): 41-42.
    Review of *Letters Home*. Compares Plath's letters to those of Virginia Woolf. The former are "simultaneously more accessible and less candid than" the latter. In both cases the letters impel readers to study the creative work of both authors, "where the true genius of each is enshrined."

56   SCHEERER, CONSTANCE. "The Deathly Paradise of Sylvia Plath." *Antioch Review* 34 (Summer): 469-80.
    Traces Plath's "anti-Edenic vision" through several of her poems. Concentrates on Plath's "garden poems" and points out that "it is always a frightening garden, one which traps without sheltering, rejects even when it entices." In her later poems, the "garden imagery" diminishes and is replaced by a "journey" metaphor. Reprinted: 1977.48.

57   SCHWARTZ, MURRAY M., and BOLLAS, CHRISTOPHER. "The Absence at the Center: Sylvia Plath and Suicide." *Criticism* 18 (Spring): 147-72.
    Presents a psychoanalytical examination of Plath's work as a way of explaining her suicide. Several clues exist in the text of the poems themselves: "She would merge with father, with mother. She would murder them. She would act out her murderous wishes. She would cope magically with the burden of actual mothering. She would end her physical pain. She would stop performing." The poems themselves reveal a psyche that has its troubled roots in Plath's early relationship with her parents. Reprinted: 1979.51.

58   SIGMUND, ELIZABETH. "Sylvia, 1926: A Memoir." *New Review* 3 (May): 63-5.
    Describes the author's close friendship with Plath in Devon. Reprinted: 1977.49 as "Sylvia in Devon: 1962."

1976

59   S[ILVEY], A[NITA]. Review of *The Bed Book. Horn Book Magazine* 52 (October): 493.
　　　This "bedtime poem" has a very "gentle quiet quality" but is less "creative than it might be."

60   STEESE, ELLEN. "Quiet Stories for Bedtime, Anytime." *Christian Science Monitor*, 3 November, p. 28.
　　　Review of *The Bed Book*. A captivating book for children, which will be "welcomed" by their parents.

61   STEINBRINK, JEFFREY. "Emily Dickinson and Sylvia Plath: The Values of Morality." *Women and Literature* 4:44-48.
　　　Presents Dickinson and Plath as "quite unlike one another," despite the fact that they are often compared. Analyzes Plath's "Lady Lazarus" and Dickinson's "Just lost, when I was saved" to demonstrate that even when they "share a vantage point or an observation, they eventually arrive at the very different conclusion."

62   "Sylvia Plath at 13 Bedford Square." *Bookseller*, 27 March, pp. 1760-62.
　　　Review of *Letters Home*. Includes excerpts in which Plath describes as 'great fun" her 1961 part-time editorial work on "the Spring and Autumn Export issues" of *Bookseller*.

63   THWAITE, ANTHONY. "'I have never been so happy in my life.': On Sylvia Plath." *Encounter* 46 (June): 64-67.
　　　Reviews *Letters Home*. The letters are in no way a substitute for a complete collection of Plath's poems. If they shed any light on the poems at all, "they do so through hints and omissions as much as through [any other] material." The letters do dispel any notion that Plath was a feminist.

64   TRUSCOTT, ROBERT BLAKE. "The Hazards of the Romance of Death: Reflections on the Poetics of Sylvia Plath and Anne Sexton." *Stone Country* 76 (Fall): 35-37.

1976

Characterizes both poets as so in love with themselves dead that death became their only identity. Because their "confessional stance" lacks the "perspectival support of either history . . . or God . . . , [they] can draw inspiration" only from the Self, and the Self as subject is far too limited to sustain them.

65 TYLER, ANNE. "'The Voice Hangs On, Gay, Tremulous.'" *National Observer* 15 (10 January): 19.
Focuses on the discrepancy between the tone of Plath's *Letters Home* and that of her work. Aurelia Plath's concern over the publication of *The Bell Jar*, which prompted her to assemble the letters, is unwarranted. The letters will be of little help to students of Sylvia Plath's work. Reprinted 1988.81.

66 WARD, DAVID. "The Good Face." *English* 25 (Autumn): 247-52.
Review essay of *Letters Home*. If Sylvia Plath had lived, we would read her poetry and her prose differently than we read it now. However, we "wouldn't be reading *Letters Home* at all." Generally, these letters to her mother "display a determination to cope and be cheerful about it . . ."

67 WHITTIER, GAYLE. "The Divided Woman and Generic Doubleness in *The Bell Jar*." *Women's Studies* 3:127-46.
Places the criticism of *The Bell Jar* into three main categories: that which labels it as "thinly-veiled autobiography"; that which "dismiss[es] its technique as that of the 'poet's novel'"; and that which "regard[s] [it] as a feminist manifesto." Discusses the reason for the "diversity" of interpretation. The "confusion" results from "the sociological shaping of [the book], for [it] is structurally deceptive and tonally deficient, at once open-ended in a contrived way and tightly narrated by its own participant, Esther Greenwood."

1977

1   ALVAREZ, A. "The Prison of Prose." *Observer*, 16 October, p. 36.
     Review of *Johnny Panic and the Bible of Dreams*. Plath's prose
is not nearly as brilliant as her poetry, even though she labored
tirelessly to perfect it. Her prose "moves stiffly, unwillingly." It lacks the
rage and sorrow of her best poetry. Still, in this volume, one gets the
"sense of a writer learning, developing, mastering the art of prose as she
had mastered that of poetry."

2   ANDREJEVIC, HELEN B. Review of *The Bed Book*. *Parents'
     Magazine and Better Housekeeping* 52 (January): 70.
     The poet creates "a deliciously nonsensical land full of
impossible but fascinating wonders no child could resist."

3   BERE, CAROL. "*Letters Home: Correspondence, 1950-1963.*" *Ariel* 8
     (October): 99-103.
     Plath's *Letters Home* will do little to change the focus of Plath
criticism from "the relationship of female creativity to madness and
suicide" to "the very real development of Sylvia Plath, the poet." The
ebullient personality presented in the letters seems to have been
deliberately created by "relatives and editors." Reprinted: 1984.2;
1988.8.

4   BIRJE-PATIL, J. "The Autobiography of a Fever: The Poetry of
     Sylvia Plath." *Indian Journal of American Studies* 5 (January and
     July): 10-20.
     Discusses Plath's poetry as "an intensely vivid experience of the
physical act of dying, realized through a sudden onslaught of brilliant
images." Instead of creating order out of chaos, Plath's art "upsets
order" and "rage[s]" for chaos.

5   BLAYDES, SOPHIE B. "Metaphors of Life and Death in the Poetry
     of Denise Levertov and Sylvia Plath." *Dalhousie Review* 57
     (Autumn): 494-506.
     Discusses the different uses of metaphor in the work of the two
poets. Both "provide insight into life and death." Plath "negates life,"

1977

while Levertov "celebrates life." Plath sees and articulates the "sickness of a sick world," while Levertov creates an "antidote for that sickness."

6   BOBBITT, JOAN. "Lowell and Plath: Objectivity and the Confessional Mode." *Arizona Quarterly* 33 (Winter): 311-18.
    Discusses the seeming paradox of "emotional disengagement" in the poetic expression of personal subject matter exhibited in the poetry of both Lowell and Plath. The tone of both is often "clinical and analytical" in spite of the autobiographical content of the poems. Just how this detachment and distancing are accomplished is explained through a close reading of several poems.

7   BROE, MARY LYNN. "Demythologizing Sivvy: That 'Theatrical Comeback in Broad Day.'" *Poet and Critic* 10:30-39.
    Views Plath's poetry in the light of the poet's own words from *Letters Home*: "'always I want to be an observer. I want to be affected by life deeply, but never so blinded that I cannot see my share of existence in a wry, humorous light and mock myself as I mock others.'" Turns the focus away from psychological criticism and "autobiographical myth."

8   ____. *Protean Poetic: The Poetry of Sylvia Plath*. Columbia: University of Missouri Press, 226 pp.
    Critical analysis of all Plath's work published up to that time. Examines both Plath's fiction and poetry in chronological order according to when it was written rather than when it was published. The author's stated purpose is to "demythologize Plath" through "a close and careful examination of [her] themes and techniques rather than [through a focus upon] the lurid details of her life."

9   BUTLER, CHRISTOPHER. "Home Journal." *Essays in Criticism* 27 (January): 77-83.
    Review essay of *Letters Home*. The book tends to discredit the view of many critics that "marital stresses and psychological depressions" were the major influences in Plath's life and work. The letters should be "put in evidence for their own sakes," not interpreted "as part of a sustained Freudian 'family romance'."

10   BUTSCHER, EDWARD. "In Search of Sylvia: An Introduction." In
      Sylvia Plath: The Woman and the Work. New York: Dodd, Mead &
      Co., pp. 3-29.
          Explores the relationship between Plath's poetry and her life.
      Reports on several of the interviews Butscher had with Plath's friends
      and family members, and discusses many of her poems at some length.

11   ____, ed. *Sylvia Plath: The Woman and the Work*. New York: Dodd,
      Mead & Co., 242 pp.
          A collection of critical essays. Contents: Richard Wilber's
      "Cottage Street, 1953"; Gordon Lameyer's "Sylvia at Smith"; Laurie
      Levy's "Outside the Bell Jar"; Dorothea Krook's "Recollections of Sylvia
      Plath"; Jane Baltzell Kopp's "'Gone, Very Gone Youth': Sylvia Plath at
      Cambridge, 1955-1957"; Clarissa Roche's "Sylvia Plath: Vignettes from
      England"; Paula Rotholz's "For Sylvia at 4:30 a.m."; Elizabeth
      Sigmund's "Sylvia in Devon: 1962"; Pamela Smith's "Architectonics:
      Sylvia Plath's *Colossus*"; Marjorie G. Perloff's "On the Road to Ariel:
      The 'Transitional' Poetry of Sylvia Plath"; Gordon Lameyer's "The
      Double in Sylvia Plath's *The Bell Jar*"; Constance Scheerer's "The
      Deathly Paradise of Sylvia Plath"; Arthur K. Oberg's "Sylvia Plath and
      the New Decadence"; Robert Phillips's "The Dark Funnel: A Reading
      of Sylvia Plath"; Joyce Carol Oates's "The Death Throes of
      Romanticism: The Poetry of Sylvia Plath."; Irving Howe's "The Plath
      Celebration: A Partial Dissent."

12   CANTRELL, CAROL H. "Self and Tradition in Recent Poetry."
      Midwest Quarterly 18 (July): 343-60.
          Whereas Lowell finds his "presence of the past" in Boston, "for
      Plath the tradition's larger, but even more confining" – that of the "long-
      suffering minority" (women, Jews). "In her work the poetic principle of
      passivity is united with enforced passivity urged on certain groups, not
      by poetic necessity, but by the distaste of society." Escape is through the
      imagination.

13   DICK, KAY. "Short Stories." *Times*, 1 December, p. 9.
          Review of *Johnny Panic and the Bible of Dreams* and five
      collections by other authors. Plath "fans" will find "little to criticize."

1977

14   DOBBS, JEANNINE. "'Viciousness in the Kitchen': Sylvia Plath's Domestic Poetry." *Modern Language Studies* 7 (Fall): 11-25.
     Interprets several poems and *The Bell Jar* in order to illustrate Plath's tendency to link "physical and mental pain" and even death with "domestic relationships and/or domestic roles. Often this suffering is presented as punishment for "doing or being bad."

15   DORAN, RACHEL S. "Female – or Feminist: The Tension of Duality in Sylvia Plath." *Transition* 1 (Winter 1977-78): 14-20.
     Discusses Plath's dual nature by comparing *Letters Home* to her poetry and prose. Although many critics have commented on Plath's split personality, "Arthur Oberg may come the closest to clarifying it as a struggle between the real and ideal self." However, he succumbs to the temptation of oversimplification. . . . "Reducing an artist's work to . . . intellectual dichotomies [means a] fail[ure] to take the chaos of human realities into account." Reality constricts women in whatever role[s] they choose.

16   EVANS, WILLIAM R. "Bell Jars: Plath and Holmes." *American Notes and Queries* 15 (March): 105-7.
     Speculates that Plath's title, *The Bell Jar*, may have come from Oliver Wendell Holmes's *The Autocrat at the Breakfast Table*. Quotes the most pertinent section of that work where Holmes asserts that "Society places its transparent bell-glass over the young woman who is to be the subject of one of its fatal experiments."

17   FRASER, G. S. "Pass to the Centre." *Listener* 98 (27 October): 541-42.
     Reviews *Johnny Panic and the Bible of Dreams: Short Stories, Prose and Diary Excerpts*. Agrees with Ted Hughes that Plath knew the stories were "sentimental *pastiche* aimed at a popular market." Says of Hughes's introduction to the collection that it was written by "a critic of the first order." Reprinted: 1988.25.

18   GILBERT, SANDRA M. "'My Name Is Darkness': The Poetry of Self-Definition." *Contemporary Literature* 18 (Autumn): 443-57.

Suggests that the "self-defining confessional genre" may be a peculiarly "female poetic mode." Although the confessional tradition can be traced back to Whitman, Yeats, Wordsworth, and Byron, "males who create mytholog[ies] of the self" can more easily turn the private into public, all the while maintaining objectively detached, because each feels certain that his "personal crisis . . . [is the] symbolic embodiment of national and cultural crisis.'" Women, on the other hand, never feel "representative," as women must "striv[e] for self-knowledge," and in the process must "experiment with different propositions" about themselves. A woman's struggle toward self-definition often means "postulat[ing] that perhaps she has not one but two (or more) selves, making her task bewilderingly complex." The poetry of five women poets (Plath, Rich, Sexton, Levertov, and Wakoski) is analyzed.

19   GLOVER, JOHN. "Re-Enter the Writer's Life." *Stand* 19:58-59.
       Review of *Letters Home*. This book is valuable for the "interesting sense of period" it gives readers. "Plath's political awareness [is] mixed with private crisis. . . . There is a pivot in her work that look[s] forward to social and political unease whilst easily looking back to the War and to the foundation of literary modernism."

20   GOTO, AKIO. "Sylvia Plath no Sekai." *Eigo Seinen* 122 (1 March): 585-87.
       Presents Plath as one of the few modern poets whose work ties the persona and the poet closely together. Despite the many negative horrific images she creates, the overall effect may be viewed as positive. She is fascinated with the tension created by opposites. Usually, however, this tension is resolved in a kind of fusion of the opposing sides. In Japanese.

21   GUTTENBERG, BARNETT. "Sylvia Plath, Myth and 'The Hanging Man.'" *Contemporary Poetry* 11 (Winter): 17-23.
       Responds to G.S. Fraser's report of his seminar's discussion "The Hanging Man" (see 1973.9) and also to Gary Martin Lane's reaction to Fraser's article (see 1975.16). Neither writer was thoroughly accurate in explaining the poem, which is autobiographical "only on the most pedestrian level." The central issue is a concern "for the fate of the poet and of the creative spirit." The poem is explicated stanza by stanza.

1977

22 HERMAN, JUDITH B. "Plath's 'Daddy' and the Myth of Tereus and Philomela." *Notes on Contemporary Literature* 7 (January): 9-10.
    Compares "Daddy" to the Myth of Tereus and Philomela. Just as the persona of the poem is unable to speak because her tongue is stuck so Philomela is unable to speak because her tongue has been cut off. She and Plath's persona are both victims of male tormenters.

23 ____. "Reflections on a Kitchen Table: A Note on Sylvia Plath's 'Black Rook in Rainy Weather.'" *Notes on Contemporary Literature* 7 (December): 5.
    Asserts that Plath's notion of everyday objects generating "an ecstasy" may have come from "Lily Briscoe's meditations in *To the Lighthouse*."

24 HOWE, IRVING. "The Plath Celebration: A Partial Dissent." In *Sylvia Plath: The Woman and the Work*. Edited by Edward Butscher. New York: Dodd, Mead & Co., pp. 225-35.
    Reprint of 1972.B12,* "Sylvia Plath: A Partial Disagreement"; 1973.15; 1975.13.

25 HUGHES, TED. Introduction to Plath's *Johnny Panic and the Bible of Dreams*. London: Faber and Faber, pp. 11-20.
    Describes Plath's prose-writing habits. She kept detailed descriptions of every day events, like a visit to a neighbor's home, its furnishings, people's clothing. Some of these descriptions may now be found in *Ariel* and in her journals. Mentions Plath's attraction to journalistic and short story writing. She was much more patient and "natural" with her poetry than with her "story-writing," which "always took place in an atmosphere of locked combat."

26 JACKSON, LAURA RIDING. "Suitable Criticism." *University of Toronto Quarterly* 47 (Fall): 74-85.
    A review article of Judith Kroll's *Chapters in a Mythology: The Poetry of Sylvia Plath* (1976.34). Contains a good deal about Plath and her work also.

27   KIRSCH, ROBERT. "Bell Jar vs. Candlelight of Hope." *Los Angeles Times*, 17 May, section 4, p. 3.
         Review of *Letters Home*. Characterizes the letters as providing a "more balanced view "of Plath than was provided by *Ariel* or *The Bell Jar*.

28   KOPP, JANE BALTZELL. "Gone, Very Gone Youth." In *Sylvia Plath: The Woman and the Work*. Edited by Edward Butscher. New York: Dodd, Mead & Co., pp. 62-63.
         Personal recollections of Sylvia Plath while she was studying at Cambridge. Presents Plath as "frantically driven to excel." Reprinted in part: 1988.46.

29   KROOK, DOROTHEA. "Recollections of Sylvia Plath." In *Sylvia Plath: The Woman and the Work*. Edited by Edward Butscher. New York: Dodd, Mead & Co., pp. 49-60.
         Reprint of 1976.35.

30   LAMEYER, GORDON. "The Double in Sylvia Plath's *The Bell Jar*." In *Sylvia Plath: The Woman and the Work*. Edited by Edward Butcher. New York: Dodd, Mead & Co., pp. 143-65.
         Focuses on Plath's use of the psychological double in *The Bell Jar*. Traces her interest in "doubles" back to her honor's thesis, a study of Dostoyevsky. Suggests that Plath's "Daddy" "is spoken by the author's evil double resenting her father's death and consequent loss of love."

31   ____. "Sylvia at Smith." In *Sylvia Plath: The Woman and the Work*. Edited by Edward Butscher. New York: Dodd, Mead & Co., pp. 32-41.
         The author recalls his brief courtship with Plath while she was at Smith College. Views her as having been driven by "her demons" to succeed academically at the expense of all other "aspects of her life." Concludes that Plath was caught up in a futile search for someone to replace the father she had lost in childhood," someone "to be both father and lover."

1977

32 LANSER, SUSAN SNIADER. "Beyond *The Bell Jar*: Women Students of the 1970's." *Radical Teacher* 6 (December): 41-44.
Discusses the fact that 1970's women students at the University of Wisconsin still relate to Esther Greenwood.

33 LEVY, LAURIE. "Outside *The Bell Jar*." In *Sylvia Plath: The Woman and the Work*. Edited by Edward Butscher. New York: Dodd, Mead & Co., pp. 42-48.
Reprint of 1973.19.

34 OATES, JOYCE CAROL. "The Death Throes of Romanticism: The Poetry of Sylvia Plath." In *Sylvia Plath: The Woman and the Work*. Edited by Edward Butscher. New York: Dodd, Mead & Co., pp. 206-24.
Reprint of 1973.B11*; 1974.17; 1974.18. Reprinted: 1985.19.

35 OBERG, ARTHUR K. "Sylvia Plath and the New Decadence." In *Sylvia Plath: The Woman and the Work*. Edited by Edward Butscher. New York: Dodd, Mead & Co., pp. 177-85.
Reprint of 1965: B9*.

36 OSHIO, TOSHIKO. "The Romantic Agony? Sylvia Plath no Jojo no Shitsu." *Eigo Seinen* 123 (July): 166-67.
Begins with a brief discussion of the confessional poets then proceeds to look at Plath from the point of view Joyce Carol Oates, Adrienne Rich, and Erica Jong. Mentions the great disparity between the Plath who wrote *Letters Home* and the Plath who wrote poetry. Everything she says in her poetry is addressed to herself, not to men, society, or history in general. Compares Plath to Dickinson in this respect. Dickinson, however, possessed joy and self-confidence; Plath's tragedy is that she ultimately could not solve the problem of the woman artist in modern society. In Japanese.

37 PERLOFF, MARJORIE G. "On the Road to *Ariel*: The 'Transitional' Poetry of Sylvia Plath." In *Sylvia Plath: The Woman and the*

Work. Edited by Edward Butscher. New York: Dodd, Mead & Co., pp. 125-42.
>Reprint of 1973.B312*.

38   PERLOFF, MARJORIE G. Review of *Letters Home*. *Resources for American Literary Study* 11 (Spring): 77-85.
>Reviews *Letters Home*. Finds truth in the letters which present Plath as a person who "*must* excel, . . . *must* be popular," and must make decisions. Plath comes through the letters as a person, who, "in Laingian terms [had] no sense of identity at all."

39   PERSCHMANN, HERMANN. "From Inside the Bell Jar." *Times Educational Supplement*, 30 December, p. 22.
>Review of *Johnny Panic and the Bible of Dreams*. This collection contains seven good short stories, six "weaker" ones, "some splendidly evocative journalism, journal excerpts, and a "sensitive and illuminating introduction by Ted Hughes."

40   PHILLIPS, ROBERT. "The Dark Funnel: A Reading of Sylvia Plath." In *Sylvia Plath: The Woman and the Work*. Edited by Edward Butscher. New York: Dodd, Mead & Co., pp. 186-205.
>Reprint of 1972.B26*; 1973.B14*.

41   REINOEHL, RON. "Sylvia Plath: Memento Mori." *Indiana Alumni Magazine* (September): 10-13.
>Describes the Plath manuscripts and letters acquired by the Lilly Library at Indiana University. The collection also includes memorabilia such as "drawings, homemade greeting cards, a baby book, paper dolls, newspaper clippings, report cards, post cards from camp, diaries, scrap books, locks of hair." All the items, even the seemingly insignificant, point to the "range of Plath's interests and the depth of her intelligence, as well as her development as a writer."

42   Review of *The Bed Book*. *Bulletin of the Center for Children's Books* 30 (February): 96.

1977

Describes the book as a "nursery extravaganza; ... a happy romp of inventive fancy."

43 Review of *The Bed Book*. *Reading Teacher* 31 (October): 22.
The verse is "imaginative" and "sophisticated." Recommended for young children.

44 Review of *Letters Home*. *Changing Times* 31 (June): 30.
Characterizes the letters as "an intimate account" of the years covering "Plath's college days until her death."

45 RIES, LAWRENCE R. "Sylvia Plath: The Internalized Response." In *Wolf Masks: Violence in Contemporary Poetry*. Port Washington, N. Y.: Kennikat Press, pp. 33-58.
Explains the violence in Plath's poems by maintaining that it is "a direct product of the violence in society." Her work can be thought of as a "remedy" for a "sick world." The poet herself capitulated only after she was convinced that "the situation was hopeless." The violence in the world around her continually insinuates itself into her personal life despite her attempts to "come to terms with it" by scrutinizing it.

46 ROCHE, CLARISSA. "Sylvia Plath: Vignettes from England." In *Sylvia Plath: The Woman and the Work*. Edited by Edward Butscher. New York: Dodd, Mead & Co., pp. 81-96.
Personal recollections of Sylvia Plath. Includes many biographical details concerning a visit the author made to Plath's Devon farmhouse in November 1962, after Plath's separation from Ted Hughes.

47 SAGE, LORNA. "Death and Marriage." *Times Literary Supplement*, 21 October, p. 1235.
Discusses Plath's short stories and notebook material in *Johnny Panic and the Bible of Dreams*. Agrees with Ted Hughes's introductory assertion that "'her dogged, year-in-year-out effort to write conventional fiction ... was like a persistent refusal of her genius.'" Reprinted: 1988.70.

48 SCHEERER, CONSTANCE. "The Deathly Paradise of Sylvia Plath." In *Sylvia Plath: The Woman and the Work*. Edited by Edward Butscher. New York: Dodd, Mead & Co., pp. 166-76.
Reprint of 1976.56.

49 SIGMUND, ELIZABETH. "Sylvia in Devon: 1962." In *Sylvia Plath: The Woman and the Work*. Edited by Edward Butscher. New York: Dodd, Mead, and Company, pp. 100-107.
Reprint of 1976.58.

50 SKARDA, PATRICIA L. "The Smith Letter: Expressions of Formlessness." *Smith Alumnae Quarterly* 68 (November):10-14.
Analyzes the letter as a literary form, focusing on the private correspondence of three Smith alumna: Sylvia Plath, Margaret Mitchell, and Anne Morrow Lindbergh. Plath's letters generally excel in form; however, during the last months of her life, when "she was near the end of her rope," the form disintegrates. Her letters, then, may to some extent mirror her "dissolution."

51 SMITH, PAMELA. "Architectonics: Sylvia Plath's *Colossus*." In *Sylvia Plath: The Woman and the Work*. Edited by Edward Butscher. New York: Dodd, Mead & Co., pp. 111-24.
Reprint of 1973.B16*.

52 STEIN, RUTH M. Review of *The Bed Book*. *Language Arts* 54 (March): 325.
The illustrations and poetry "match tempos – a sense of repose at beginning and end, bouncy in the middle."

53 TROMBLEY, STEPHEN. Review of *Letters Home*. *Critical Quarterly* 19 (Summer): 93-96.
The letters give rise to "contradictions, ... gaps, ... [and] inconsistencies" when read with Plath's poetry. Perhaps the most essential letters are omitted.

1977

54   UROFF, MARGARET DICKIE. "Sylvia Plath and Confessional
      Poetry: A Reconsideration." *Iowa Review* 8 (Winter): 104-15.
          Asserts that Plath's poetry is not confessional. M. L. Rosenthal
      used the term to describe Robert Lowell's work and all poetry in which
      the persona "point[s] to the poet himself." Plath's poems, however, are
      not this autobiographically realistic. Instead, her autobiographical
      details are used "emblematically." Thus, the "speakers" in her poems
      and their relationship to the past must be re-examined. Several poems
      are discussed, and the conclusion is that "they confess nothing. . . . In
      fact . . . they erect a barricade against self-revelation."

55   WAGNER, LINDA W. "Plath's 'Ariel': 'Auspicious Gales.'"
      Concerning Poetry 10 (Fall): 5-7.
          Begins by commenting on the tendency of critics to misread
      Plath's work and by asserting that Plath's heavy reliance on "archetypal
      imagery" allows many of her poems to be read as either bleak and
      despairing or hopeful by "affirmative." Concludes with an explication of
      "Ariel," an ambiguous poem whose main "image patterns [are]
      movement-stasis, light-dark, earth-fire." Establishes correspondences
      between the images in the poem and the source of the title,
      Shakespeare's character in *The Tempest*.

1978

1   BARNARD, CAROLINE KING. *Sylvia Plath*. Boston: Twayne, 132
     pp.
          Maintains that while Plath's early poetry was "amateur," it does
     contain all the concerns and themes expressed more expertly in the
     later poems. Especially evident are "fascination with death . . .,
     ambivalence toward sex, wifehood, and motherhood [,and] propensity
     to nightmare." The development of these early images and concerns is
     traced through the transitional and final poems as is Plath's use of
     "sound, structure, . . . rhythm, and language."

2   BERMAN, JEFFREY. "Sylvia Plath and the Art of Dying: Sylvia
     Plath (1932-1963)." *University of Hartford Studies in Literature*
     10:137-55.

Speculates that Plath may have found the bell jar image in H. D.'s *Tribute to Freud*, published in 1945 as "Writing on the Wall." Plath was "ambivalent toward psychotherapy [which] coincides with her tangled feelings toward art." Discusses her psychiatric history and attributes "much of her illness" to her inability to admit "the aggression she felt . . . [especially] . . . toward her mother."

3   BLOW, SIMON. "Sylvia Plath's Prose." *Books and Bookmen* 23 (June): 42-43.
Reviews *Johnny Panic and the Bible of Dreams*. The collection is of no interest except perhaps for its "technical fascination." Plath achieves objectivity and distance in only one story, "The Fifteen-Dollar Eagle." The rest are death-obsessed, just as she was. The only value of her prose is the light it sheds on her poetry, her "rightful medium."

4   BUTLER, CHRISTOPHER. "Sylvia Plath's Prose." *New Review* 4 (December 1977/January 1978): 68-69.
Review of *Johnny Panic and the Bible of Dreams*. The collection will interest critics of Plath's poetry because it exposes the author as "a major creative artist subduing herself to alien modes of speech and a tired series of generic expectations in her readers."

5   DECKER, SHARON D. "I Have a Self to Recover." *Michigan Occasional Paper* 7 (Fall), 21 pp.
Discusses the "collision" of Plath's experience as "artist, crafter of words" and her experience as "woman, wife, . . . mother, a sexual being." Plath's difficulty in resolving the conflict was due in part to her own conventional image of what a woman should be.

6   DITSKY, JOHN. Review of *Letters Home. Southern Humanities Review* 12 (Winter): 75-76.
Gives a brief synopsis of the contents of the letters. Of the 500 pages of letters, in only 40 of them do we "grow accustomed to the downward plunge toward death."

1978

7 GILBERT, SANDRA M. "'A Fine, White Flying Myth': Confessions of a Plath Addict." *Massachusetts Review* 19 (Autumn): 585-603.

Presents as the core of Plath's myth the pattern of movement from enclosure or suffocation to liberation by a "maddened or suicidal . . . avatar of the self." The poems are attempts to discover the cause of the entrapment and the way to freedom. Ironically, however, freedom is also often a trap: "One may be renewed like a baby in the warm tomb of the mythic oven, but the oven is also Auschwitz, Dachau. . . ." Reprinted: 1979.21.

8 HILL, DOUGLAS. "Living and Dying." *Canadian Forum* 58 (June-July): 32-33.

Discusses *Johnny Panic* as a valuable addition to the Plath canon. In this volume even Plath's "conventional pose" is successful. The major drawback of the collection is that "there's not enough of it." Takes a strong stand against Aurelia Plath and Ted Hughes having "exclusive responsibility of deciding what the world is to know." Argues for the "complete publication" of Sylvia Plath's work. Reprinted: 1984.18; 1988.32.

9 JUHASZ, SUZANNE. "'The Blood Jet': The Poetry of Sylvia Plath." In *Feminist Criticism: Essays on Theory, Poetry, and Prose*. Edited by Cheryl L. Brown and Karen Olson. Metuchen, N. J. and London: Scarecrow Press, pp. 111-30.

Reprint of 1976.30.

10 ___. Review of *Johnny Panic and the Bible of Dreams*. *Library Journal* 103 (15 December): 2522.

The stories are important because they show Plath's "short-circuiting her own genius" as a poet in her attempt to become a successful writer of fiction. The stories provide biographical information well; however, "read for their own sakes, they are often tedious."

11 KAZIN, ALFRED. *New York Jew*. New York: Alfred A. Knopf, pp. 326-27, 358.

1978

Recalls the creative writing class Kazin taught in which Sylvia Plath was a student. At that time, eight years before her suicide, she wrote slick, "coolly professional" prose, but nothing interesting. "There was not a line, not a thought, not a word that the magazine business would have changed." Her writing would not become electrifying "until she faced her fascination with her own death."

12 KELLY, CONOR. Review of *Crossing the Water* and *Winter Trees*. *Studies: An Irish Quarterly Review* 67 (Spring/Summer): 118-21.
      Crossing the Water both "echoes *The Colossus*" and "fore-shadows *Ariel*." By the time she wrote the poems in *Winter Trees*, "her voice had attained its distinctive pitch." Although the poems in these two volumes are not as stunning as those in *Ariel*, they do allow us to see how and out of what the *Ariel* poems evolved.

13 KING, P. R. "'Dying Is an Art': The Poetry of Sylvia Plath." In *Nine Contemporary Poets: A Critical Introduction*. London and New York: Methuen, pp. 152-89.
      Approaches Plath's work as the kind of literature which makes heavy "demands upon the reader" because its subject is the self "at its most naked and vulnerable moments." Plath's experience of all external reality was "coloured entirely by [her] sense of her own fragile identity." Focuses primarily on *The Colossus* and *Ariel*, concluding that the "poems express a collapse of identity, and yet their language, imagery and rhythm have a paradoxical zest and energy of life."

14 LANE, GARY, and STEVENS, MARIA. *Sylvia Plath: A Bibliography*. Metuchen, N. J. and London: Scarecrow Press, 144 pp.
      Contains both primary and secondary sources and a chronology of Plath's work according to dates of publication.

15 LEGARS, BRIGITTE. "La poésie selon Sylvia Plath." *Le Monde*, 4 August, p. 15.
      Plath's celebrity as an author began with the publication of *The Bell Jar*, but the marvelous progress of her writing during the last years of her life deserves more attention. Discusses *Ariel* and, briefly, *Letters Home*. In French.

1978

16 McCANN, JANET. "Sylvia Plath's Bee Poems." *South and West: An International Literary Magazine* 14:28-36.

Analyzes the five bee poems in *Ariel*. They represent a stance toward Plath's father that is the opposite of that represented in "Daddy." In the former, Plath seems to be arguing that "[her father] is good; [she is] not her father," but "must incorporate" him into her life and go on living. This attitude is in stark contrast to the one displayed in "Daddy." There, Plath merges with her father and thus must die in order to rid herself of him. The five bee poems, taken together, also show the poet's "fascination with the creative principle, her fear of it, her attempts to master and incorporate it, and her final failure to deal with it adequately."

17 MARCUS, JANE. "Nostalgia Is Not Enough: Why Elizabeth Hardwick Misreads Ibsen, Plath, and Woolf." *Bucknell Review* 24:157-77.

Plath's life and her novel, *The Bell Jar*, are inseparable from her poetry. In her work she "has harnessed hatred." She cannot rightly be called a feminist. Still, "the hatred of men . . . cannot be condoned on the grounds of the poet's style." Reprinted: 1978.18.

18 ____. "Nostalgia Is Not Enough: Why Elizabeth Hardwick Misreads Ibsen, Plath, and Woolf." In *Women, Literature, and Criticism*. Edited by Harry R. Gavin. Lewisburg: Bucknell University Press, pp. 157-77.

Reprint of 1978.17.

19 MARKEY, JANICE. Review of *Johnny Panic and the Bible of Dreams*. *Archiv für das Studium neueren Sprachen und Literaturen* 215:421-22.

Calls the collection a "valuable aid to the understanding and evaluation of the work of a great and controversial writer." Ted Hughes's decision to include some of Plath's journalistic pieces is unfortunate as they tend "to disturb the whole balance of the book."

20 NANCE, GUINEVARA A., and JONES, JUDITH P. "Doing away with Daddy: Exorcism and Sympathetic Magic in Plath's Poetry." *Concerning Poetry* 11:75-81.

Psychoanalytical analysis of "Daddy" and, to a lesser extent, "Lady Lazarus" and other *Ariel* poems. Plath uses the language and images of psychology, religion, and magic to produce a "chronological sequencing of . . . recollections of childhood, . . . through the twenty-year-old's attempted suicide to the point at thirty when the woman tries to extricate herself from her image of daddy." Reprinted: 1984.27.

21 NGUYN THAN-BINH. "A Stylistic Analysis of Sylvia Plath's Semantics." *Language and Style* 11 (Spring): 69-81.
Analyzes the semantic pattern of "Fever 103." Calls the poem "an extreme instance of Plath's utilization of semantic features for the purpose of giving a logical articulation to a poem whose content develops along a line which does not coincide with common logic. The technique used, feature surfacing, ensures a continual connection between underlying and surface level, and thus semantically relates the series of dreamlike images which constitute the poem." A chart on pages 76-79 shows word and image connections.

22 "Non-Fiction." *Observer*, 16 April, p. 27.
Review of *Letters Home*. Despite the heavy editing, there are "passages of brilliant . . . description and much that is moving."

23 OBERG, ARTHUR K. "Sylvia Plath: 'Love, love, my season.'" In *Modern American Lyric: Lowell, Berryman, Creeley, and Plath*. New Brunswick, N. J.: Rutgers University Press, pp. 127-73.
Traces "the attempts of Plath's poems to establish lyric and love and the counter movement toward elegy and to a deadly journey which could not be stopped." *Crossing the Water* and *Winter Trees* do not "contradict but extend what the *Ariel* poems were about."

24 REILLY, ERLINE. "Sylvia Plath: Talented Poet, Tortured Woman." *Perspectives in Psychiatric Care* 16 (May-June): 129-36.
Focuses on the importance of "the coincidence of pregnancy and a change in the quality and content of [Plath's] work." The rage that she turned into poetry during the last years of her life comes from "the demands of poet become mother." When her art could no longer

1978

contain the "massive upsurge of fury," Plath killed herself "rather than destroy the sanctity of motherhood."

25 Review of *Johnny Panic and the Bible of Dreams*. *Booklist* 75 (1 December): 57.
   Although these pieces do not deserve publication on their own merit, they are valuable because they "offer clues to their author's obsessions. . . ." If this volume fails as literature, it succeeds as history.

26 Review of *Johnny Panic and the Bible of Dreams*. *British Book News* (January): 57.
   The quality of the volume is, at best, mixed, "showing nothing like the talent of [Plath's] poetry or of *The Bell Jar*."

27 Review of *Johnny Panic and the Bible of Dreams*. *Kirkus Reviews* 46 (1 November): 1230.
   In her short stories as in her poetry, Plath bares her soul and scrutinizes despair. "Her problem was that she had a *Mademoiselle* mind and a *New Yorker* ambition."

28 Review of *Johnny Panic and the Bible of Dreams*. *Publishers Weekly* 214 (6 November): 71.
   The reverse chronological order in which these pieces are presented is disappointing to those who want to study Plath's development. The themes she explores are familiar, but the exploration of them in *The Journals* are "freer and more vivid" than in these stories.

29 ROSENTHAL, M. L., and GALL, SALLY M. "Pure? What Does It Mean? Notes on Sylvia Plath's Poetic Art." *American Poetry Review* 7 (May-June): 37-40.
   Analyzes several poems and concludes that they were all written *in extremis*. They "transcend personal expression while carrying their suicidal set . . . into a state of impersonal, aesthetically realized 'perfection.'"

30 RUBENSTEIN, ROBERTA. "Sylvia Plath: Uneven Fragments of an 'Inner Biography.'" *Chicago Tribune*, 24 December, section 7, p. 3.

Review of *Johnny Panic and the Bible of Dreams*. With some striking exceptions, the pieces are "closer to ideas for stories than fully realized aesthetic wholes."

31 SALOP, LYNNE. *Suisong*. New York: Vantage Press, 81 pp.

Examines the connections between "creativity and suicide." The first chapter offers an overview of several artists who committed suicide and a summary of several philosophical descriptions of creativity by Arieti, Wertheimer, Koestler, Freud, Barron, Jung, Seidel, Coleridge, Kierkegaard, and others. The second chapter is a biographical essay on Plath. The remaining chapters examine Plath's torment, despair, depression, and movement toward suicide as seen through her work.

32 SCHVEY, HENRY. "Sylvia Plath's *The Bell Jar*: *Bildungsroman* or Case History." *Dutch Quarterly Review of Anglo-American Letters* 8:18-37.

Disagrees with Plath criticism which "threatens to obscure the quality of the writing with biographical detail." Some critics romanticize her suicide as "a glorious act of artistic fulfillment." Others see her "art as the product of a schizoid personality, and therefore false and dangerous." Examines *The Bell Jar* as a work of art which is not dependent on the details of its author's . . . biography.

33 SIMPSON, LOUIS. "Black, Banded with Yellow." In *A Revolution in Taste: Studies of Dylan Thomas, Allen Ginsburg, Sylvia Plath, and Robert Lowell*. New York: Macmillan, pp. 85-127.

A biographical essay which shows Plath's poems as growing directly out of the events in her life. However, as her later poems attest, her work makes "an impression that cannot be accounted for by looking to their sources in mythology or the life of the poet." In the end "her art is complete and distinct from her life." Published simultaneously in England by Collier Macmillan as *Studies in Dylan Thomas, Allen Ginsburg, Sylvia Plath, and Robert Lowell*.

1978

34   SMITH, STAN. "Never Forgetful Witnesses: David Holbrook on Sylvia Plath." *New Blackfriars* 59 (March): 112-22.

Takes issue with David Holbrook in his second chapter of *Sylvia Plath: Poetry and Existence* (see 1976.28). Gives Holbrook credit for his assertion that "Sylvia Plath's language is radically *overdetermined*" but charges him with taking an "over-literary" approach and with pursuing a "primarily didactic" purpose. Accuses him of suggesting "remedies [which] . . . are proscriptive and authoritarian."

35   SRIVASTAVA, NARSINGH. "Anti-Self in the Poetry of Sylvia Plath." *Literary Criterion* 13:36-43.

Explores the "fusion of antithetical motifs" in Plath's poetry, especially in *Ariel*. "Plath's extremist mode of excitement owes to a violent invasion of the ideal over the real." Uses a psychological approach to show how the violence of the fusion leads to the "[deep] complexity" found in her poems.

36   THOMPSON, JAN. Review of *Johnny Panic and the Bible of Dreams*. *Ambit* 73:88-89.

Characterizes the stories as stiff and artificial because in her strained attempt to be objective, Plath "sacrificed everything central to observation and detailed description." However, her prose contains the same "vision of emptiness and alienation" as her poetry.

37   TOOMEY, PHILIPPA. "In Search of Sylvia." *Times*, 8 April, p. 11.

Review of *Letters Home*. Presents brief biographies of Aurelia, Otto, and Sylvia Plath. Contains many of Aurelia's comments about her daughter's life and about the misreading of her work by the public.

1979

1   ACHARYA, SHANTA. "An Analysis of Sylvia Plath's 'Edge.'" *Literary Criterion* 14:52-57.
      Explicates "Edge" as one example of Plath's ability to "deal with the most mystical elements of existence without sacrificing any precision of craftsmanship."

2   AIRD, EILEEN M. "'Poem for a Birthday' to 'Three Women': Development in the Poetry of Sylvia Plath." *Critical Quarterly* 21 (Winter): 63-64.
      Traces Plath's development as a poet from "Poem for a Birthday" to "Three Women." Comments on the influence of Roethke and Lowell. In the *Ariel* poems "the very experience of pain is the means by which the persona grows to a new power: the first statement of this is in 'Poem for a Birthday.'" Reprinted: 1988.1.

3   ATKINSON, MICHAEL. "After Twelve Years, Plath without Tears: A Look Back at 'Lady Lazarus.'" In *A Book of Rereadings in Recent American Poetry – 30 Essays*. Edited by Greg Kuzma. Lincoln, Nebr.: Pebble Press, pp. 301-9.
      Speaks of the poem's persona as "Plath": "What we have here is not, of course, Plath as she was, but a fictive Plath in the process of becoming a dramatic presence in her own imagination – and ours." The poet envisions herself as the "muse's opposite," thus leaving us "terrified and mute." Reprinted: 1979.4.

4   ___. "After Twelve Years, Plath without Tears: A Look Back at 'Lady Lazarus.'" *Pebble* 18-20:301-9.
      Reprint of 1979.3.

5   ATWOOD, MARGARET. "'Johnny Panic,' the Last Prose." *Los Angeles Herald Examiner*, 11 February, p. E-11.
      Reprinted with different title: 1979.6.

6   ___. "Poet's Prose." *New York Times Book Review*, 28 January, p. 10.

1979

Reviews *Johnny Panic and the Bible of Dreams*. This volume will appeal mainly to those who have read the rest of Plath's work, for they will recognize the "foreshadowings, cross-references, influences and insights. . . ." Even in the most frivolous stories, Plath's "own emotional mainsprings" come through. Notes the significance of the chronologically reversed order of the arrangement of the stories. Reprinted with different title: 1979.5.

7   BEDIENT, CALVIN. "Sylvia Plath, Romantic. . . ." In *Sylvia Plath: New Views on the Poetry*. Edited by Gary Lane. Baltimore and London: Johns Hopkins University Press, pp. 3-18.
   Finds Plath's intensity and tendency toward "reaction" part of the romantic tradition. Explains how her poems are actually subjective dramas. "She herself was the drama." Her "struggle against fear, pain [and] isolation" is undeniably romantic.

8   BERE, CAROL. Review of *Johnny Panic and the Bible of Dreams*. *Southern Humanities Review* 13 (Fall): 358-60.
   The collection "illustrates . . . that Plath had immense difficulties converting observed fact into memorable fiction." She views her characters with a detached aloofness; "there is a frightening cold-bloodedness to her approach."

9   BLESSING, RICHARD ALLEN. "The Shape of the Psyche: Vision and Technique in the Late Poems of Sylvia Plath." In *Sylvia Plath: New Views on the Poetry*. Edited by Gary Lane. Baltimore and London: Johns Hopkins University Press, pp. 57-73.
   Discusses the late poems in terms of their structure, style, and tone, and comments on Roethke's influence. "Plath's great and underlying terror is always the nausea of movement itself." She achieves velocity and horror through a clever use of ambiguity and imagery. What emerges in the poetry is a movement "from dominance to submission and back, less a matter of rebirth than of escape and mastery and bondage and escape again."

10   "Books in Brief: *Johnny Panic and the Bible of Dreams*." *Critic* 37 (15 March): 7.

1979

Review of *Johnny Panic*. Each story is imprinted with typical Plathian characteristics: "terrible controlled force [and] autobiographical premonitions of disaster." Compares Plath's "almost too terse" control to that of Flannery O'Connor.

11   BROE, MARY LYNN. "'Oh Dad, Poor Dad': Sylvia Plath's Comic Exorcism." *Notes on Contemporary Literature* 9 (January): 2-4.
        Contends that while digging for "autobiographical 'facts,'" critics have missed the humor in Plath's "Daddy." The poem is a "mock-exorcism ritual that . . . backfires on the exorcist."

12   BUTLER, C. S. "Poetry and the Computer: Some Quantitative Aspects of the Style of Sylvia Plath." *Proceedings of the British Academy* 65:291-312.
        Examines the findings of a computer analysis of Plath's style and its development over four volumes of poetry: *The Colossus, Crossing the Water, Ariel,* and *Winter Trees*. The types of data fed into the computer concern vocabulary, word length, punctuation, number of end-stopped and run-on lines, number and length of sentences, numbers of contractions, and syntactic patterns. The results verified the initial hypothesis: "[T]he poems of *The Colossus* showed a somewhat stilted, formally complex style, while the late poems were more informal and colloquial in tone."

13   CONGER, JOHN. "Moral Growth and Alienation." In *Adolescence – Generation under Pressure*. New York: Harper and Row, pp. 102-6.
        Discusses suicide among the young and uses Plath's suicide as an example of an act "intended simply as a gesture." She did not mean to kill herself, for she left a note explaining how to reach the doctor, and she knew her baby-sitter would arrive soon.

14   COSGRAVE, MARY SILVA. Review of *Johnny Panic and the Bible of Dreams*. *Horn Book Magazine* 55 (April): 220.
        The value of the collection lies in its illumination of the "themes and symbols that later emerged in *The Bell Jar* and in the

1979

poems of *Ariel*." Although its prose is "substantial and fresh," it does not measure up to her poetry.

15   "Current Publications." *Smith Alumnae Quarterly* 71 (November): 26.
      Review of *Johnny Panic and the Bible of Dreams*. A sampling of Plath's best short stories, journalistic pieces, and journal excerpts.

16   DOWIE, WILLIAM. "A Season of Alarums and Excursions: *Johnny Panic and the Bible of Dreams*." *America* 140 (3 March): 165-66.
      Reviews *Johnny Panic*, and calls Plath the "quintessential observer," a fact verified in her notebooks as well as in her poetry and stories. Her descriptions of people, however, though sharp and accurate, are flat, lacking in emotional involvement. Her stories, like her diary, are "cold as ice." The title story is the best of the collection because it deals with the only subject about which Plath does not write dispassionately – death.

17   ELLIOT, HARVEY. "Sylvia Plath: Living a Death Poem." *After Dark* 12 (May): 76-79.
      Gives a detailed account of the autobiographical aspects of *The Bell Jar* and the struggle out of which the novel grew. Published at the time of the release of the motion picture, *The Bell Jar*.

18   FERRIER, CAROLE. "The Beekeeper's Apprentice." In *Sylvia Plath: New Views on the Poetry*. Edited by Gary Lane. Baltimore and London: Johns Hopkins University Press, pp. 203-17.
      Presents a feminist reading, focusing especially on the bee poems. The poetry repeatedly expresses the same dilemma, the two choices women raised in a patriarchal culture are offered: "self-destruction or motivation toward revolutionary social change." Plath's last work represents an effort to make her personal experiences universally significant.

19   GELPI, BARBARA CHARLESWORTH. "A Common Language: The American Woman Poet." In *Shakespeare's Sisters: Feminist*

1979

Essays on Women Poets. Edited by Sandra M. Gilbert and Susan Gubar. Bloomington: Indiana University, pp. 269-79.

Explores the issue of victimization in connection with American women poets and outlines several responses of women poets *to* victimization. Plath acknowledges victimization but considers it an act of fate, perhaps unavoidable because of the dictates of biology or necessity. Her response is often a hatred of men, mother, woman, body, and self. "Her doom is to be a woman, both her condition and her conditioning swallowing her up."

20 GILBERT, DEBORAH. "Transformations in 'Nick and the Candle-stick.'" *Concerning Poetry* 12 (Spring): 29-32.

Concentrates on the persona's transformation from an attitude of despair to one of affirmation. The change is convincing because of the carefully controlled poetic imagery, which "reflects [the speaker's] emotional progress." Discusses the "sexual, alchemical, religious, and evolutionary" images specifically and comments on the significance of "the poem's highly controlled stanzaic form."

21 GILBERT, SANDRA M. "'A Fine, White Flying Myth': The Life/Work Sylvia Plath." In *Shakespeare's Sisters: Essays on Women Poets*. Edited by Sandra M. Gilbert and Susan Gubar. Bloomington: Indiana University Press, pp. 245-60.

Reprint of 1978.7.

22 GILES, RICHARD F. "Plath's 'Maudlin.'" *Explicator* 37 (Summer): 24-26.

Explains Plath's "Maudlin" as a retelling of the poet's loss-of-virginity experience, made applicable to all women.

23 GUTTENBERG, BARNETT. "Plath's Cosmology and the House of Yeats." In *Sylvia Plath: New Views on the Poetry*. Edited by Gary Lane. Baltimore and London: Johns Hopkins University Press, pp. 138-52.

Establishes correspondences between Yeats and Plath. Both "hammer[ed] [their] thoughts into [the] unity [of a] ... complete system." Plath began this process early and despite "significant departures from Yeats," a pattern very like his appears. Similarities in imagery are also obvious, but Plath's final vision was much darker than Yeats's.

24   HAUSSER, LEOLA. Review of *Johnny Panic and the Bible of Dreams*. *Best Sellers* 39 (June): 105.
       Questions the wisdom of publishing this prose work which is far inferior to Plath's poetry. *Letters Home* was a more important contribution to Plath's literary reputation. Calls Ted Hughes's introduction "clinically objective."

25   HOMBERGER, ERIC. Review of *Johnny Panic and the Bible of Dreams*. *Journal of American Studies* 13 (August): 281-82.
       Plath's "relentless" effort to succeed as a short story writer whose work is published by the *New Yorker* did not succeed. The stories in this volume "are artistically of a lower order altogether than her poems."

26   JENKINS, PAT. "Understanding Sylvia Plath." *Cleveland Magazine* 8 (October): 30, 32.
       Discusses a local theatre director's perceptions of Plath as she prepares to direct a stage production of *Sylvia Plath, A Dramatic Portrait*.

27   KENNER, HUGH. "Sincerity Kills." In *Sylvia Plath: New Views on the Poetry*. Edited by Gary Lane. Baltimore and London: Johns Hopkins University Press, pp. 33-44.
       Contends that *The Colossus* showed much promise but that its formalism "detained [Plath's] mind upon the plane of craft, and so long as it was detained there it did not slip toward what beckoned it." The "bogus spirituality" of *Ariel* confirms that the promise of *The Colossus* was never realized.

28   LANE, GARY. "Influence and Originality in Plath's Poems." In *Sylvia Plath: New Views on the Poetry*. Edited by Gary Lane. Baltimore and London: Johns Hopkins University Press, pp. 116-37.

Traces the course of Plath's "early imitative phase" pointing out specific places where she mimics other poets, then moves on to describe and discuss "the originality of the voice Plath finally made her own." Names Thomas, Stevens, Roethke, and Yeats as the major influences on her work. The voice she eventually developed by "casting off" her mentors was triggered by her appendectomy in 1961 and is first heard in "Tulips." This voice is "original and of sustained intensity."

29 ____. Introduction to *Sylvia Plath: New Views on the Poetry*. Baltimore and London: Johns Hopkins University Press, pp. ix-xiv.

Briefly discusses past Plath criticism, dividing it into three stages. The first, which focused on *The Colossus* and *The Bell Jar*, was (and Mary Kinzie is quoted here) "brief, reserved, entirely conventional.'" The second stage "was devoted to re-evaluation and canonization"; the third raised Plath to "something very like poetic sainthood." In addition, each of the essays in the collection is briefly summarized.

30 ____, ed. *Sylvia Plath: New Views on the Poetry*. Baltimore and London: Johns Hopkins University Press, 264 pp.

A collection of critical essays. Contents: Calvin Bedient's "Plath, Romantic . . . "; J. D. McClatchy's "Short Circuits and Folding Mirrors"; Hugh Kenner's "Sincerity Kills"; David Shapiro's "Sylvia Plath: Drama and Melodrama"; Richard Allen Blessings's "The Shape of the Psyche: Vision and Technique in the Late Poems of Sylvia Plath"; J. D. O'Hara's "Plath's Comedy"; Sister Bernetta Quinn's "Medusan Imagery in Sylvia Plath"; Gary Lane's "Influence and Originality in Plath's Poems"; Barnett Guttenberg's "Plath's Cosmology and the House of Yeats"; Marjorie Perloff's "Sylvia Plath's 'Sivvy' Poems: A Portrait of the Poet as Daughter"; Murray M. Schwartz and Christopher Bollas's "The Absence at the Center: Sylvia Plath and Suicide"; Carole Ferrier's "The Beekeeper's Apprentice"; and Jerome Mazzaro's "Sylvia Plath and the Cycles of History."

31 LEIDER, EMILY. "Sylvia Plath and Superman." *San Francisco Review of Books* 5 (June): 23-24.

Reviews *Johnny Panic and the Bible of Dreams*. Discusses Plath's relationships with her father and her husband, and recommends

1979

that *Johnny Panic* . . . be read "along with *Letters Home* and *The Bell Jar* as background for the poems."

32   LOVE, ANN BURNSIDE. "The Legend of Plath, the Scent of Roses." *Washington Post*, 29 April, pp. N-1, 6-7.
   Reports on the reunion of the women who were guest editors of *Mademoiselle* with Plath. Includes reminiscences about Plath and reactions to the recently released film based on *The Bell Jar*.

33   McCLATHCHY, J. D. "Short Circuits and Folding Mirrors." In *Sylvia Plath: New Views on the Poetry.* Edited by Gary Lane. Baltimore and London: Johns Hopkins University Press, pp. 19-32.
   Points to Plath's "rapidly evolving relationship to style" as her most important quality as a poet. Discusses this evolution from her early poems (*The Colossus*) through her last ones (*Ariel*). Sees Plath as willing to experiment "with voice and the relationships among tone and image and address," placing her on the same level as Lowell and Roethke.

34   McCLAVE, HEATHER. "Sylvia Plath: Troubled Bones." *New England Review* 2:447-65.
   Discusses the significance of Plath's experiencing self as "emptiness." It becomes "in her poetry as in her life, a total environment, and suffocating and protective at once." Objects are important to Plath only "as correlative for her private responses." Her "psychic paralysis" prevents objectivity. She "install[s]" herself as "the center of things," then abandons that peace. Without herself as center, her world falls apart. Plath is compared to Dickinson, Whitman, Stevens, and T. S. Eliot. Judith Kroll's book (1976.34) is also mentioned.

35   McLELLAN, JOSEPH. "Sylvia Plath and the Landscape of the Soul." *Washington Post*, 19 January, p. D-6.
   Review of *Johnny Panic and the Bible of Dreams*. Most readers of this volume will be looking for autobiographical material, and they will find it. The stories range from "masterpieces to unabashed potboilers." In many instances fact and fiction are so intertwined that a

reader can see how one becomes the other. The best story in the collection is "Stone Boy with Dolphin."

36   MAZZARO, JEROME. "Sylvia Plath and the Cycles of History." In *Sylvia Plath: New Views on the Poetry*. Edited by Gary Lane. Baltimore and London: Johns Hopkins University Press, pp. 318-40.

Discusses the era in which Plath lived, including the cultural, literary, political, and scientific issues that shaped her interests and attitudes, and found their way into her poetry. The influences of other writers (Lowell, Roethke, and Eiseley) are also explored. Reprinted with slight revision: 1980.12.

37   MINER, VALERIE. "A Poet's Fateful Journey." *San Francisco Chronicle*, 18 February, "This World" section, p. 58.

Review of *Johnny and the Bible of Dreams*. Characterizes Plath's tone in the volume as "distinct from her haunting poetry." Here Plath shows herself to be "a writer of wit, irony and charm."

38   O'HARA, J. D. "Plath's Comedy." In *Sylvia Plath: New Views on the Poetry*. Edited by Gary Lane. Baltimore and London: Johns Hopkins University Press, pp. 74-96.

Begins with a general discussion and definition of comedy and of comic incongruity in particular, then proceeds to place Plath within this definition. The personae of her poems may have "abnormal sensibility," and thus often elicit "kindly responses" from readers. At the same time, however, Plath's speakers are "self-assured, perhaps even ... deliberately amusing." Thus, they leave readers unsure of their own responses. This dis-ease is the root of Plath's brand of black humor, which exploits "the disparity between pain and appearance."

39   PERLOFF, MARJORIE. "Beyond *The Bell Jar*: Women Poets in Transition." *South Carolina Review* 11 (Spring): 4-16.

Begins with a discussion about the differences between women's and men's poetry, maintaining that such a difference does exist, although it is difficult to describe or define. Women seem to rely on metaphors more than men do. As Plath herself admitted in a 1958 letter to her brother: "My main difficulty has been overcoming a clever,

1979

too brittle and glossy feminine tone, and I am gradually getting to speak 'straight out,' and of real experience, not just in metaphorical conceits." Concludes by pointing to several of today's women poets who rely on "tough," violent metaphors as Plath did, but do not have "the vision that stands behind [them]."

40   ___. "Sylvia Plath's 'Sivvy' Poems: A Portrait of the Poet as Daughter." In *Sylvia Plath: New Views on the Poetry*. Edited by Gary Lane. Baltimore and London: Johns Hopkins University Press, pp. 55-78.

Argues that Plath's "schizoid personality" was responsible for the disparity between the self she presented in *Letters Home* and her early poems and that which emerges in *Ariel*. Traces the transformation from the former to the latter self through a biographical account, and explains Plath's early poetry on the basis of her relationship with her mother. Concludes by asserting that "Sivvy" finally becomes Sylvia through "independence from her husband and mother," but that the "assertion 'there is nothing between [them]' could only mean that now there would be nothing at all."

41   POLLITT, KATHA. "Aesthetic Suicide." *Harper's Magazine* 258 (February): 83-86.

Review of *Johnny Panic and the Bible of Dreams*. Mourns the fascination feminists seem to have with suicides by women authors. Instead of exulting in successes, these feminists "cherish . . . breakdowns and self-destruction. . . ." This volume is not a success. In fact, it is hard to believe that Plath spent any of her considerable creative energy on stories like these. The explanation is that "Plath appeased the contradictory requirements of her character by a complex system of double-entry literary bookkeeping." *The Bell Jar*, her poetry and diaries clearly express her doubts about her "ability to lead a normal life." At the same time, her letters and "commercial fiction" are used to deny those doubts.

42   QUINN, BERNETTA. "Medusan Imagery in Sylvia Plath." In *Sylvia Plath: New Views on the Poetry*. Edited by Gary Lane. Baltimore and London: Johns Hopkins University Press, pp. 97-115.

1979

Explicates Plath's "Medusa," broadening the explanation to encompass the Medusan imagery in other poems as well. "[T]ropology in ["Medusa"] moves from (1) jellyfish to (2) Gorgon to (3) the lunar Muse over art conceived of as 'sculpted form' to (4) the 'false heaven' of drugs as counteractive to the emotional disorders that led to her suicide."

43   ROBERTSON, NAN. "Death and the Wronged Mother." *San Francisco Chronicle*, 25 October, p. 43.
        Contains Aurelia Plath's comments insisting that *The Bell Jar* was not autobiographical. *Letters Home* proves that Mrs. Plath and her daughter had a solid, loving relationship. Reprinted with a different title: 1979.44.

44   ____. "*Letters Home* Binds Plath Mother-Daughter." *Chicago Tribune*, 11 November, section 12, p. 9.
        Reprint of 1979.43.

45   ROSENBLATT, JON. "Sylvia Plath: The Drama of Initiation." *Twentieth Century Literature* 25 (Spring): 21-36.
        Repudiates the notion that Plath's poetry is exclusively confessional. Instead her work should be read as the "play[ing] out [of] the dramatic conflict between opposed external forces on the field of the poet's body and self." This conflict often takes place in a "symbolic space" to which the persona must travel and in which the two ides merge in a "ritual confrontation." Using the imagery of ancient rites, Plath creates a "poetry of initiation" through which the "self and body are transformed." This rite is analyzed stage by stage through a discussion of several poems.

46   ____. *Sylvia Plath: The Poetry of Initiation*. Chapel Hill: University of North Carolina Press, 180 pp.
        Analyzes many of Plath's poems by applying the concept of "initiatory structure," which is Rosenblatt's term for the pattern of death and rebirth that often appears in the poems. Maintains that Plath was influenced by Paul Radin's *African Folktale and Sculpture*.

1979

47   ROSENBLUM, HARRIET S. "Another Sampling of Plath Legacy."
Democrat and Chronicle, 4 February, p. G-2
        Review of *Johnny Panic and the Bible of Dreams*. The book
may offer a corrective to the excessively effusive and "severely edited"
Letters Home and the "hack psychoanalysis" of Edward Butscher's
biography (see 1976.11). These short stories do not flatter Plath. "She
was clearly not born a storyteller."

48   ROSENSTEIN, HARRIET. "Remembering Sylvia Plath: 16 Years
after Her Death." *Los Angeles Herald Examiner*, 11 February, pp. E-
11.
        Reprint of 1972.B30*. Original title: "Reconsidering Sylvia
Plath."

49   SACHAR, NEVA NELSON. "The Real Story Behind *The Bell Jar*."
Mademoiselle 85 (March): 112, 114.
        Reports on the reunion of the 1953 *Mademoiselle* guest editors
on the occasion of the release of the movie version of *The Bell Jar*.

50   SAROT, ELLIN. "To Be 'God's Lioness' and Live: On Sylvia Plath."
Centennial Review 23 (Spring): 105-28.
        Explores Plath's "understanding of 'confessional' art." Though
it has its roots in the poetry of Lowell and Sexton, Plath's
confessionalism developed along different lines from theirs.

51   SCHWARTZ, MURRAY M., and BOLLAS, CHRISTOPHER.
"The Absence at the Center: Sylvia Plath and Suicide." In *Sylvia
Plath: New Views on the Poetry*. Edited by Gary Lane. Baltimore and
London: Johns Hopkins University Press, pp. 179-202.
        Reprint of 1976. 57.

52   SHAPIRO, DAVID. "Sylvia Plath: Drama and Melodrama." In
Sylvia Plath: New Views on the Poetry. Edited by Gary Lane.
Baltimore and London: Johns Hopkins University Press, pp. 45-53.
        Plath's poetry is overwritten, "over-determined, . . . and
referential." Her better poems are those, like "Tulips," that do not "bolt

toward death," yet much of Plath's work is "stubborn, irreducible melodrama."

53 STORHOFF, GARY P. "Plath's Comic Mode in 'You're.'" *Notes on Contemporary Literature* 9: 8-10.

Discusses the poem as a rather rare example of Plath's happy and even conventional sensibilities. In "You're" she "depicts herself as the typical mother-to-be, undisturbed by existential pain and doubt." The poem is witty and humorous; its metaphors combine "to become elaborate jokes."

54 THWAITE, ANTHONY. "Out of the Quarrel: On Sylvia Plath." *Encounter* 53 (August): 40-44.

Takes issue with those who want to make Plath into a "legend." If they succeed, they will "falsify and diminish her." Far too much speculation, gossip, and rumor is published as Plath criticism. Uses Edward Butscher's biography of Plath (1976) as one example. Also mentions Margaret Dickie Uroff's *Sylvia Plath and Ted Hughes* (1979.35), calling it a "sober, sane, and on the whole jargon-free book."

55 UDAYAKUMAR, K. "Treatment of Death in the Poetry of Sylvia Plath." *Literary Half-Yearly* 20 (July): 12-20.

Draws on Plath's biography and poetry to show that "although her general theme is the dialectic of life and death, she concentrates more on death as she proceeds." She views death ambivalently, at first with more emphasis on its terror. Gradually, however, she comes to "love its final repose."

56 UROFF, MARGARET DICKIE. "On reading Sylvia Plath." *College Literature* 6 (Spring): 121-28.

Explores the tendency of both students and critics of Plath to focus on "the raw experiences [her work] purportedly contains," while ignoring the "carefully structured text[s]." This approach results in a severely limited understanding of the poet. A more fruitful approach is to read *as poems*, not as biography.

1979

57   ____. *Sylvia Plath and Ted Hughes*. Urbana: University of Illinois
Press, 235 pp.
Assesses the relationship of Plath and Hughes and explores its
effect upon their work. Many of the characteristics of Plath's work that
some critics have labelled "pathological" are actually only
manifestations of Plath's and Hughes's common interest in "magic,
myth, nature and violence."

58   ZIVLEY, SHERRY LUTZ. "Plath's Family Album: Portraits of
Grotesques." *Ball State University Forum* 20:74-79.
Discusses the angry and hateful poetic portraits Plath paints of
her family members. Although those focusing on her father are the
most well-known, she also "indict[s] her mother, husband, aunt and
even children and an uncle-in-law." Some readers conclude that Plath
"manifests Freudian psychosis" in these portraits; others, that the
pressure to be a perfect wife, mother, and artist was so overwhelming
that it left Plath "embittered against those she loved."

1980

1   ANNAS, PAMELA J. "The Self in the World: The Social Context of
Sylvia Plath's Late Poems." *Women's Studies* 7 (1980): 171-83.
The violent, shocking images of the *Ariel* poems are "only the
end result of an underlying depersonalization, . . . and an economic and
social structure that equates people and objects." Women are more
"alienated and dehumanized" than men. Compares Plath's position to
that of Marx. Quotes and briefly discusses Frederic Jameson in relation
to Plath's concerns in her late poems. Reprinted: 1984.1.

2   BROE, MARY LYNN. "A Subtle Psychic Bond: The Mother Figure
in Sylvia Plath's Poetry." In *The Lost Tradition: Mothers and
Daughters in Literature*. Edited by Cathy N. Davidson and Esther M.
Broner. New York: Frederick Ungar, pp. 217-30.
Explores the relationship between Plath and her mother by
examining *Letters Home* and much of Plath's poetry, especially *Crossing
the Water*. "Sylvia and Aurelia Plath both wasted so much time in hand-
maiden tasks. . . . They confused creative identity with romantic
involvement, yet neither recognized the crippling fact in the other." In

her poetry, Plath consistently attempts to discover the effect of "a matrilineal bond" on her life as a poet.

3   DAVIDSON, JANE. *The Fall of a Doll's House: Three Generations of American Women and the Houses They Lived In*. New York: Holt, Rinehart, and Winston, pp. 141-201 passim.
      Chronicles the author's friendship with Plath when they were both students at Smith College. Sets the events of Plath's life in a historical context.

4   FAAS, EKBERT. "Lady Lazarus." In *Ted Hughes: The Unaccommodated Universe*. Santa Barbara: Black Sparrow Press, pp. 73-75.
      Begins by citing studies which reveal that "current methods of diagnosing and treating mental illness" are similar to those of witchcraft. Introduces Sylvia Plath into the discussion by focusing on the electroshock therapy she received at age 21. The experience was shattering and it gave rise to much of Plath's subsequent poetic imagery. The purpose of the discussion is to show how Plath's experiences affected Ted Hughes's work.

5   GARDNER, PHILIP. "'The Bland Granta': Sylvia Plath at Cambridge." *Dalhousie Review* 60 (Autumn): 496-507.
      Presents a history of Plath's publishing successes and failures at Cambridge from 1955 to 1957, observing that perhaps "her recognition by Cambridge had come too late for her to care about it." Discusses the influence of other poets and of Cambridge magazine editors on her work during those years.

6   HARGROVE, NANCY DUVALL. "Sylvia Plath." In *Dictionary of Literary Biography: American Novelists since World War II*. Second Series. Vol. 6. Detroit: Gale Research Company, pp. 259-63.
      Calls *The Bell Jar* "a forerunner of such works as Erica Jong's *Fear of Flying* and Marilyn French's *The Women's Room*." Because the novel is so autobiographical, some knowledge about Plath's life is essential to understanding the book. Presents a biographical sketch and shows how Plath's personal experiences are represented in the novel.

1980

Places it with Salinger's *Catcher in the Rye* and Joyce's *A Portrait of the Artist as a Young Man*.

7   HEJE, JOHAN. *Key to Sylvia Plath: The Bell Jar*. Copenhagen: Munksgaard, 87 pp.
    Provides study aids especially for college students reading *The Bell Jar*. Includes only such biographical material as will illuminate the autobiographical aspects of the novel. Concludes with "Comprehension Questions and Vocabulary" and "Subjects for Oral or Written Work."

8   HUGHES, TED. "Sylvia Plath." In *Ted Hughes: The Unaccommodated Universe*, by Ekbert Faas. Santa Barbara: Black Sparrow Press, pp. 180-82.
    Reprint of "Notes on the Chronological Order of Sylvia Plath's Poems": 1966.B1*; 1970 B.2*.

9   JOHNSON, GREG. "A Passage to 'Ariel'": Sylvia Plath and the Evolution of Self." *Southwest Review* 65 (Winter): 1-11.
    Asserts that those critics who label Plath's poetry "confessional," have "misinterpreted" her work. They have focused so much upon Plath's life that they have "minimized the importance of her art." In fact, Plath has, from the beginning, emphasized "artistic transformation rather than personal confession. Several poems are analyzed closely.

10 KROLL, JUDITH. "Plath, Sylvia." In *Notable American Women: The Modern Period*. Edited by Barbara Sicherman, et al. Cambridge, Mass.: Belknap Press, pp. 49-60.
    A brief biography of Plath that includes her publishing history. Makes some connections between her life and her work.

11 MALLON, THOMAS. "Sylvia Plath's 'Insomniac' and the British Museum." *Notes on Modern American Literature* 4 (Fall): 25-26.
    Presents a close reading of Plath's poem "Insomniac" and speculates that "there may be more to tie it to the British Museum than ... evidence that it was composed there. ... Plath may have been

1980

influenced not only by the museum's architecture, but by Virginia Woolf's earlier prose descriptions of the museum and the neighborhood surrounding it."

12   MAZZARO, JEROME. "The Cycles of History: Sylvia Plath." In *Postmodern American Poetry*. Urbana: University of Illinois Press, pp. 139-65.
        Reprint of 1979.36 Slightly revised.

13   MORI, KUNIO. "Sylvia Plath as a Poet in the Sixties." In *The Traditional and the Anti-Traditional: Studies in Contemporary American Literature*. Edited by Kenzaburo Ohashi. Tokyo: Tokyo Chapter, American Literary Society of Japan, pp. 103-7.
        Maintains that Plath became a "true poet" only after abandoning the "credos of modernism" to which she adhered as a young poet. Her early poems faithfully display the "poetics of modernism"; however, once she gained confidence in her own voice, she moved toward a "deeply personal poetry with a new style. . . ." What she retained of modernism was a "conservative attitude toward . . . form."

14   Review of *Johnny Panic and the Bible of Dreams*. *New York Times Book Review*, 3 February, p. 33.
        Documents Plath's "strengths and weaknesses" and provides evidence of "her conviction that 'poetry was an evasion'" of the real work of writing fiction.

15   VENDLER, HELEN. "Sylvia Plath Playing Pygmalion to Her Own Galatea." In *Part of Nature, Part of Us: Modern American Poets*. Cambridge, Mass.: Harvard University Press, pp. 271-76.
        Reprint (without the title) of 1971.B57*.

16   WILHELM, ALBERT E. "Sylvia Plath's 'Metaphors.'" *Notes on Contemporary Literature* 10:8-9.
        Suggests that even in a witty poem like "Metaphors" the speaker exhibits an "ambivalent attitude toward her sex and the blessing

1980

or curse of pregnancy." Discusses the mixed messages conveyed by some of the poem's images.

1981

1   BAYLEY, JOHN. "Games with Death and Co." *New Statesman* 102 (October): 19-20.
    Review of *The Collected Poems*. Compares Plath's talent with Marianne Moore's and Elizabeth Bishop's. Seen as part of Plath's process of development, the *Ariel* poems "no longer seem the revelation they seemed . . . after the poet's death."

2   BOSWORTH, PATRICIA. "Sweet Revenge." *Working Woman* 6 (December): 112-13.
    Review of *The Collected Poems*. Includes a brief biography of Plath. Concludes that this volume makes it difficult to separate the author's genius from "the horror and fascination of her suicide."

3   BRADLEY, DEBRA. "Smith Acquires Papers of Poet Sylvia Plath." *Daily Hampshire Gazette*, 17 September, p. 1.
    Reports on Smith's purchase of Plath's literary collection, certain parts of which "will be sealed for 50 years" to protect those people still living who are mentioned in Plath's writing.

4   BRAUCH, M. RUTH. "'A Self to Recover'–Sylvia Plath." *Delta Kappa Gamma Bulletin* 47 (Summer): 20-25.
    Discusses the influences on Plath's work of the Imagist poets, of her family, and of the pressure to "pursue her art, while struggling to meet life in the terms traditionally prescribed for womanhood."

5   CLARK, TOM. "Raw Nerves at the Cabaret of Despair." *San Francisco Chronicle*, 11 October, "Review," p. 4.
    Review of *The Collected Poems*. The volume allows us finally to assess Plath's genius as it developed over the years. Her last poems show her "formal skills . . . reaching a peak, but they were at the service of internal disorder." The chronological ordering of the poems allows

1981

us to see Plath's death as "not only foretold in, but demanded by, her poetry."

6   DONOGHUE, DENIS. "You Could Say She Had a Calling for Death." *New York Times Book Review*, 22 November, pp. 1, 30-31.
          Reviews *The Collected Poems*. Plath's art, as well as her life, suffered from her "self-absorption." The most intense poems and those full of rage are not as good as those "that live without fuss, poems in her middle style . . . often poems of pure observation." The landscape poems are especially admirable. Reprinted with different title: 1987.4.

7   DUTTA, UJJAL. "Poetry as Performance: A Reading of Sylvia Plath." *Literary Criterion* 16 (1981): 1-11.
          Emphasizes the importance of judging Plath as a poet on the basis of her poetry alone, without the intrusion of biographical details. Her work succeeds only when she is able to "organize [confessional] pressures into an independent experience, into poetic action, at once personal and impersonal." This achievement is seldom evident in her work.

8   HULSE, MICHAEL. "Formal Bleeding." *Spectator* 247 (14 November): 20.
          Pronounces *The Collected Poems* "the most important volume of the last 20 years." Plath's primary strength is her ability to filter strong emotional responses through the intellect. Reprinted: 1988.36.

9   JACOBSEN, JOSEPHINE. Sylvia Plath and Anne Sexton: Enduring Poetic Voices." *Washington Post*, 22 November, "Book World" section, p. 6.
          Review of *The Collected Poems* by Plath and *The Complete Poems* by Sexton. Since Plath's poems are so often about death, it is impossible to read them without considering her suicide. Compares and contrasts the two poets and concludes that Plath's work was "less marred by the exigencies of her struggle."

1981

10   KAMEL, ROSE. "'Reach Hag Hands and Haul Me In': Matrophobia in the Letters of Sylvia Plath." *Northwest Review* 19:198-208.
   Letters Home reveals as much about Aurelia as about Sylvia
Plath. Suggests that Sylvia saw "her mother as a Doppelgänger, a
double, undermining her sense of herself as a separate being." The
letters reveal that Sylvia internalized her mother's anxieties and values,
and that she was both appalled by and attracted to the Doppelänger
staring back 'from the mercury-backed glass' with 'hag hands waiting to
haul [her] in.'" Reprinted: 1988.40.

11   KILGORE, KATHRYN. "Rituals of Self-Hatred, Arts of Survival."
Village Voice Literary Supplement 3 (December): 20, 30.
   Review of *The Collected Poems*. The chronological order of
the poems has "destroyed the coherence of Plath's separate volumes."
Her style was completely developed at age 24 and did not change much
during her remaining years. "Her focus on the self, the self, the self"
also remained the same as did her love for "clean language [over] what
it failed to convey."

12   MARTIN, ELAINE. "Mother, Madness, and the Middle Class in
The Bell Jar and *Les mots pour le dire*." *French-American Review* 5
(Spring): 24-47.
   Examines the similarities and differences in two women's
novels about "madness," Plath's *The Bell Jar* and Marie Cardinal's *Les
Mots pour le dire*. Although one author is American and the other
French, the novels offer us "two sides of a single madness, a madness
that has its roots in external elements but can only be uprooted through
internal strengths."

13   MOSS, HOWARD. "Dying: An Introduction." In *Whatever Is
Moving*. Boston: Little, Brown & Co., pp. 176-82.
   Reprint of 1971.B41*. Reprinted: 1985.17.

14   MOSSBERG, BARBARA ANTONIA CLARKE. "Sylvia Plath." In
*American Women Writers: A Critical Reference Guide from Colonial
Times to the Present*. Vol. 3. Edited by Lina Mainiero and Langdon
Lynne Faust. New York: Frederick Ungar, pp. 395-98.

1981

A biographical essay, including a brief discussion of most of Plath's work. Emphasizes the ways in which "[t]he facts of P[lath]'s biography inform her writing."

15   NYE, ROBERT. "Poetry." *Times*, 22 October, p. 11.
    Review of *The Collected Poems*. Disagrees with those who judge Plath a "minor poet" because many of her poems are "less powerful" than those in *Ariel*. That she worked to perfect her craft underscores her enormous talent.

16   ORGEL, SHELLEY. "Fusion with the Victim: A Study of Sylvia Plath." In *Lives, Events, and Other Players: Directions in Psychobiography*. Edited by Joseph T. Coltrera. New York: Aronson, pp. 123-72.
    Reprint of 1974.20. Title changed slightly.

17   PERLOFF, MARJORIE. "Sylvia Plath's *The Collected Poems*." *Resources for American Literary Study* 11 (Autumn): 304-13.
    Laments the control Ted Hughes has exercised over the publication of Plath's work and disagrees with his inclusion of fifty "juvenalia" poems written before 1956. Refutes the "now-fashionable judgment" that her early poems are as important as those in *Ariel*. Gives several examples of Plath's poetry to show the influence of Hopkins, Yeats, Auden, Wilbur, Stevens, Dylan Thomas, Lowell, Roethke, and Hughes. Reprinted: 1988.62.

18   PRITCHARD, WILLIAM H. "An Interesting Minor Poet?" *New Republic* 185 (30 December): 32-35.
    Discusses *The Collected Poems* of Sylvia Plath. Notes the "confusion" about Sylvia Plath that was caused by the "piecemeal" publication of her work before this volume was released. Views Plath as having moved from a "rigid formal structure" in the earlier poems to more "fluidity of motion" and emotion in the later ones. Reprinted: 1984.32; 1988.66.

1981

19   Review of *The Collected Poems*. *Booklist* 78 (15 September): 74.
       Includes Plath's successes and failures and proves beyond any
doubt that *Ariel* was her finest work.

20   Review of *The Collected Poems*. *Kirkus Reviews* 49 (15 September):
       1229.
       The interest in this volume is generated for the most part by
the poet's suicide. The collection "fill[s] out our picture of Plath's
development, but fails ... to justify the ... claims implied by such a
comprehensive presentation." Plath's ambition was stronger than her
achievement.

21   Review of *The Collected Poems*. *Publishers Weekly* 220 (16 October):
       66.
       The chronological presentations of the poems allows one to
"follow the poet's progress and stylistic changes." The "haunting images"
were created by a "mind made restless by the everyday, undone by
childbirth, imbued with a tragic inevitability and eventual desire for
death."

22   RICKS, CHRISTOPHER. "The Black Luck of Sylvia Plath." *Sunday
       Times*, 11 October, p. 42.
       Review of *The Collected Poems*. "Her poems are not only
about obsessions but are obsessive." Notes the significance of the way
"each poem take[s] up at least one word ... from the previous poem."
This technique images forth one of Plath's own fears: "'small, mean and
black,/ Every little word hooked to every little word.'"

23   ROSEN, LOIS. "Sylvia Plath's Poetry about Children: A New
       Perspective." *Modern Poetry Studies* 10:98-115.
       Focuses on the poems in which "children are used in basic
image patterns." The poems are especially important because Plath's
best poems were written during the time when she was raising her own
children. In addition, Plath herself said that "the real issues in our time
are the issues of every time – children, loaves of bread, paintings,
building; and the conservation of life of all people in all places." Gives a
close analysis of several poems.

1981

24 SANAZARO, LEONARD. "Sylvia Plath and the Borestone Mountain Poetry Awards: 1955-1963." *Notes on Contemporary Literature* 11 (September): 2-3.

Notes that Plath won sixteen *Borestone* poetry awards during the years 1955-1963. Lists each award-winning poem and the dates and places of their original publication.

25 SCHAEFFER, SUSAN FROMBERG. "Plath's Poems Resurrect Her from Shadows of Myth." *Chicago Tribune*, 20 December, section 7, pp. 1, 5.

Review of *The Collected Poems*. Decries those myth-making readers who view Plath as a literary "Marilyn Monroe or Judy Garland." This volume will undo much of the sensationalism that has surrounded its author, allowing readers to see that her poetry "negates the pain of the events from which they rise." Perhaps the most helpful aspect of the book is the chronological ordering of the poems.

26 SKEI, HANS. "Sylvia Plath's 'Lady Lazarus': An Interpretation." *Edda* 81: 233-44.

Discusses "Lady Lazarus" as one part of Plath's late work, all of which is actually "one continuous poem in which the themes, images, and structuration are very similar and relatively limited." Plath blends "her private agony" with world events which she sees as "violent, threatening, and destructive." Thus, her personal poetry becomes "at once less private and . . . more relevant." The poet's biography is useful for interpreting the work but must be used "extremely cautiously." "Lady Lazarus" is not "dependent on the events of the poet's life."

27 SRIVASTAVA, AVADESH K. "The Intense Flame: Letters and Poems of Sylvia Plath." *Indian Journal of American Studies* 11 (January): 71-81.

Discusses *Letters Home* and several poems as representing two very different sides of Plath's psyche. Her poetry is death-haunted. In it "a notion develops . . . that the poet seeks death because she loves life."

28 WAGNER, LINDA W. "45 Mercy Street and Other Vacant Houses." In *American Literature: The New England Heritage*. Edited

by James Nagel and Richard Astro. New York and London: Garland, pp. 145-65 passim.

Places Plath within the poetic tradition begun by Dickinson, Emerson, Thoreau, and Whitman. Plath and Sexton, like their forerunners, place their poems "much more directly in the province of the heart than in any [geographical] location." Focuses on Plath's "sense of alienation and her search for a "place" in which she can feel secure as a "'rebel'" and an "'artist.'" That she felt more at ease in England and near the sea is substantiated in her work. "For all her emphasis on endurance, Plath's poems leave us rather with the anguish, the sense of displacement, the search for place, the terrible weight of responsibility."

29 WEATHERS, WINSTON. *The Broken Word: The Communication Pathos in Modern Literature*. New York: Gordon and Breach Science Publishers, pp. 199-203.

Mentions Plath as part of a discussion about "the issue of death and suicide in contemporary American poetry." These artists are examples of "the use of the word, not as an instrument of communication but ... of personal psychic therapy." Plath's suicide altered her readers' perceptions of even her very early work.

30 WITTLINGER, ELLEN. Review of *The Collected Poems*. *Library Journal* 106 (1 November): 2142-43.

Serves to remind members of the Plath cult that "the woman behind the myth was indeed a brilliant writer." Even the very earliest poems display her tremendous talent.

31 ZIVLEY, SHERRY. "Plath's Will-Less Women." *Literature and Psychology* 31:4-14.

Discusses the psychological consequences of regression into "will-lessness," which the female personae in many of Plath's poems exhibit. "Many [of them] ... manifest serious schizophrenic symptoms. ..." The poet's "recurring images" of Jews in concentration camps, hospital patients, prisoners, and queen bees in hives convey a sense of "frustration, helplessness, and fury." In most cases the personae are women victims suffering from the domination of "male tyrants."

1982

1 BERESFORD, ANNE. "Sylvia Plath." *Agenda* 19-20 (Winter-Spring): 109-11.

   Review of *The Collected Poems*. The chronological ordering of the poems allows the reader to see Plath develop from a "wordy and . . . labored" to an "unencumbered style."

2 BONNER, THOMAS, J. "Plath's Journals Link Author's Private Life to Her Fiction." *New Orleans Times-Picayune*, 13 June, section. 3, p. 14.

   Review of *The Journals*. Their "literary quality rivals" that of Plath's imaginative work. Many of the events that eventually found their way into *The Bell Jar* are found here.

3 BROWNJOHN, ALAN. "A Way Out of the Mind." *Times Literary Supplement,* 12 February, pp. 165-66.

   Review of the *Collected Poems*. The volume "provides an opportunity to follow [Plath's] scrupulous process of assess[ing]" her own work. Her adept handling of images is her "most original contribution to poetry."

4 BURTON, DEIRDRE. "Through Glass Darkly: Through Dark Glasses: On Stylistics and Political Commitment – via a Study of a Passage from Sylvia Plath's *The Bell Jar*." In *Language and Literature: An Introductory Reader in Stylistics*. Edited by Ronald Carter. London: Allen and Unwin, pp. 195-214.

   Argues for a new stylistics that admits that observation and description "of phenomena [cannot be done] in a 'neutral' and 'objective' way." Since "there is no conceivable 'a-political' work in this or any other society," it is the responsibility of linguists and literary critics to "examine and act upon the poetical implications of literature." Analyzes a section of *The Bell Jar* to provide a model for helping students understand "the ways in which language constructs the 'reality' of everyday life. . . . So that . . . everyday 'reality' can usefully be seen as a series of 'fictional' constructs – as texts open to analysis and inter-pretation . . . just . . . as texts marked out for literary study are."

1982

5   CLEMONS, WALTER. "A Poet's Rage for Perfection." *Newsweek* 99 (3 May): 77.
    Review of *The Journals*. Comments on the "cheery, false-face Plath presented to the world and on the degree to which Plath's journals give the lie to such a front. Recommends *The Journals* to "any aspiring writer" because it shows "how unremittingly she work[ed]."

6   COTTER, JAMES FINN. Review of *The Bell Jar*. *America* 146 (February): 157-58.
    The section of poems for this volume is impressive, and Ted Hughes's comments "most helpful" for a deeper understanding of the "depths [that] remain hidden beneath the surface of these strange poems."

7   DAVIE, DONALD. "Cambridge Theatre." *London Review of Books* 4 (19 August-1 September): 17.
    Review of *The Collected Poems*. Plath is the "patent-holder" for our time of poetry as theatre, as "emotional drama."

8   DAVISON, PETER. Letter to the editor. *Washington Post*, 30 May, "Book World" section, p. 14.
    Takes issue with Frances McCullough's letter (1982.26). Plath accused many people besides Davison of being jealous of her work. *Letters Home* and *The Journals* speak for themselves on that topic. The real scandal is the deplorable manner in which Plath's work has been published. The crucial question is, "who has profited" from this publishing history? Davison suggests that Ms. McCullough knows the answer.

9   ____. "Sylvia Plath: Consumed by the Anxieties of Ambition." *Washington Post*, 18 April, "Book World" section, pp. 3, 11.
    Review of *The Journals*. Mentions the vast difference between the Plath of this book and the Plath of *Letters Home*. Plath shows herself to be concerned with success above all. This book is a relatively unimportant part of the Plath canon. She herself would likely be unhappy with its being published.

10   DICKIE, MARGARET. "Sylvia Plath's Narrative Strategies." *Iowa Review* 13 (Spring): 1-14.

Explores Plath's tendency to combine the "narrative" and "lyric modes" in her poetry. Maintains that her ability to create a "narrating lyric" is evident in her early work and that it can be traced throughout her later work as well. Identifies recurring "plots" within several poems. Reprinted 1984.10.

11   DULHAMEL, P. ALBERT. "Sylvia Plath: Always on Stage." *Boston Herald American*, 9 May, p. B24.

A review of *The Journals*. These diary entries portray a Plath who constantly evaluated her everyday "successes and failures," but seldom admits her own intense "ambition and egotism." Unfortunately any such admissions have been edited out. These omissions are a great detriment to the book.

12   EDER, DORIS L. "Lady Lazarus Two Decades Later: Sylvia Plath's *Collected Poems*." *Denver Quarterly* 17 (Spring): 105-11.

A review essay. *The Bell Jar* allows the reader to assess all Plath's poetry and to see "how far and fast she progressed within her brief lifespan." Her reputation rests rightly upon *Ariel*. Discusses the characteristics of the early, middle, and late poems. In spite of her desire to make her work "relevant to other things," it remains narrow in scope, "utterly self-centered." Still, "her art . . . remains beautiful and vital" despite its limitations.

13   EHRENPREIS, IRVIN. "The Other Sylvia Plath." *New York Review of Books* 29 (4 February): 22-24.

A review of *The Collected Poems*. Plath's best poems consistently "dramatize the willed effort of the human identity to establish itself." Quotes from several poems to illustrate "syntax, figures of speech, and modes of expression," all of which are evidence of the poet's "double vision of moral reality." The struggle for identity is exacerbated by the ambiguous, confusing signals it received "from the environment."

1982

14   GILES, RICHARD F. "Plath's 'Maudlin.'" *Explicator* 40 (Spring):
       56-59.
            Establishes correspondences between Plath's own experiences
       with Dick Norton at Boston's Lying-In Hospital and the images in
       "Maudlin." Also draws upon Plath's chronicling of these experiences in
       The Bell Jar.

15   GLACKIN, WILLIAM C. "A Writer Who Had to Write." *Sacramen-*
       to Bee, 28 March, "Scene" section, pp. 1, 6.
            A biographical essay that explores Plath's need to write. Also
       reviews a stage performance of *Letters Home*.

16   GRAVIL, RICHARD. Review of *The Collected Poems*. *British Book*
       News (February): 112-13.
            Presents Plath as a 'minor poet' whose poems, nevertheless,
       evince "both craft and passion." The evolution of Plath's technique and
       voice is discussed.

17   GRIFFIN, SUSAN. "The Public Rage and Private Hell of Sylvia
       Plath." *San Francisco Chronicle*, 18 April, "Review" section, p. 8.
            A review of *The Journals*. Discusses the ways in which *The Bell*
       Jar articulates women's struggle for independence and identity.
       However, it was the deep conflict within herself that finally defeated
       Plath. She wanted to be not only the all-American girl, but also wife
       and mother, as well as the perfect "scholar, teacher," and writer. Her
       journals "give us a record of her continual labor toward sanity and
       survival."

18   GROSHOLZ, EMILY. "*The Collected Poems*: Sylvia Plath." *Hudson*
       Review 35 (Summer): 319-33.
            Review of *The Collected Poems*. Plath endeavored to change
       the brand of impurity "which society places on women. Many of her
       poems express the conflict between the pure and impure often
       symbolized by the colors red and white. Finally, however, "her strategies
       are inadequate . . . [and she sinks] into the Ultimate Solution."

1982

19   HUCKABY, MARY PJERROU. "Plath: Present at the Creation."
Los Angeles Times, 3 January, "Book Review" section, p. 7.
Review of *The Collected Poems*. The book is valuable for its
chronological ordering of the poems. Ted Hughes should have been
less an editor and more a commentator, however. More information in
certain places would have been helpful.

20   ___. "Plath's about Ready for Benign Neglect." *Los Angeles Times*,
30 May, "Book Review" section, p. 6.
Review of *The Journals*. The context is mostly "banal, confused,
and overwritten." Questions the critical attention Plath receives. These
journals represent the poet at her worst, and much of the editorial
cutting of the text is "absurd."

21   JACKSON, MARNI. "In Search of the Shape Within." *Maclean's
Magazine*, 17 May, p. 57.
Reviews *The Journals*. Maintains that although there are
scholarly motives for a close study of *The Journals*, most readers are
looking for clues to Plath's suicide. In either case an in-depth look at
the poet is prevented by Plath's husband, mother, and by the book's
general editor, Frances McCullough. What does come through in *The
Journals* is Plath's total "vulnerability." Reprinted: 1988.37.

22   KLOSS, ROBERT J. "Further Recollections on Plath's 'Mirror.'"
University of Hartford Studies in Literature 14:11-22.
Discusses Plath's "Mirror" by answering the question Plath
poses in "Three Women." "What is it I miss?/Shall I ever find it,
whatever it is?" What she misses is adequate mirroring of the mother
during infancy. "Mirror" contains "rage, . . . separation anxiety, . . . [and]
the desire to remain fused." All are explained by Plath's very early
relationship with her mother.

23   LARKIN, PHILIP. "Horror Poet." *Poetry Review* 72 (April): 51-53.
Reviews *The Bell Jar*. Judges Plath's early poems to be
uninteresting, especially lacking in form. By 1959, her style is imitative
of Roethke's and the change is "shock[ing] and sudden." Although she is
exerting more control over her material by this time, the pleasure of

1982

reading her poetry is "nullified by the nature of that material and her involvement with it." Her last poems are "jauntily impersonal; it is hard to see how she was labelled confessional." Reprinted: 1983.12.

24   LERNER, LAURENCE. "Sylvia Plath and the Others: New Poetry." *Encounter* 58 (January): 53-54.
        Expresses appreciation to Ted Hughes for his "care and tact" in editing *The Collected Poems*. Disagrees with the argument that Plath's "early work is controlled, formal, . . . superficial. . . . The late poems . . . are imbued with a new power." Sees the later poems as also controlled, but in a different way. Many poems would fit into *Ariel*. Reprinted: 1984.21; 1988.50.

25   L[OO], M[ICHAEL] D. Review of *The Collected Poems*. *Kliatt Young Adult Paperback Book Guide* 16 (April): 26.
        Although Plath's early work is uninteresting, "all of her mature works are worthwhile." Comments on the ironic fact that had Plath lived, her work may have been eclipsed by that of her husband; instead, Ted Hughes now lives in her shadow, "[his] career built on the genius and notoriety of a dead wife."

26   McCULLOUGH, FRANCES. "Sylvia Plath." *Washington Post*, 30 May, "Book World" section, p. 14.
        A letter to the editor responding to an earlier letter by Peter Davison. Maintains that Davison displays "personal bias." Plath herself had said that "he was jealous of her work." Contradicts Davison's claims that the Hughes family had not cooperated with the author of the only authorized biography.

27   McDOWELL, EDWIN. "Time Capsule: 2013." *New York Times Book Review*, 14 November, p. 34.
        Notes the opening of the Sylvia Plath Collection at the Smith College Library rare book room.

28   M[EADE], M[ARION]. Review of *The Journals*. *Ms.* 10 (June): 76, 80.

1982

Criticizes Ted Hughes for omitting so much material from the book. What is left is important as "literary history," but is actually a portrait of Plath which has been "laundered and ironed."

29 MILFORD, NANCY. *"The Journals of Sylvia Plath."* New York *Times Book Review*, 2 May, pp. 1, 30-32.
       Quotes extensively from *The Journals*. Concludes that Plath's journals "are dominated from the first by the twin threats of sex and vocation." Expresses anger about the editorial cuts made by Ted Hughes. Reprinted: 1984.24.

30 MORAMARCO, FRED. "'Burned-Up Intensity': The Suicidal Poetry of Sylvia Plath." *Mosaic* 15 (Winter): 141-51.
       Argues against the notion that Plath's suicide is irrelevant to a serious study of her work. Her "suicidal fixation" can be seen even in *The Colossus*, which most critics regard as merely "carefully crafted technical exercises." Plath's suicide *is* relevant, "even central to our understanding of the work." Reading Sylvia Plath as a "suicidally obsessed" poet who expressed her obsession through her work does not "minimize" her artistic genius.

31 MUDRICK, MARVIN. "Tales of Waste and Woe." *Hudson Review* 35 (Autumn): 460-70.
       Review essay on *The Journals*. The entries have an air of artificiality about them. "[Plath] writes what she thinks a writer ought to write who will grow up to be worthy of publication in *The New Yorker*." Lengthy excerpts from journal entries and poems are included.

32 NEWENHUYSE, ELIAZBETH CODY. Review of *The Journals*. *Christian Century* 99 (26 May): 638.
       This collection shows Plath to be "difficult [and] complicated"; innocent, but full of "shadowed hungers."

33 PETTINGELL, PHOEBE. "The Voices of Sylvia Plath." *New Leader* 65 (May): 10-11.

1982

> Review of *The Journals*. The voice found here is the same one "that controls the poems of *Ariel*." Outlines a "progression of startling transformations" in the life of the poet and reiterates the theme of rebirth so often found in the poems.

34 POLLITT, KATHA. "A Note of Triumph." *Nation* 234 (16 January): 52-55.

> Begins by citing several critics' views of Sylvia Plath. These responses are faulty because they are based on her suicide, not on her actual work. *The Collected Poems* will improve her reputation among her critics. It provides "evidence [of a] broadly continuous [artistic] development." Reprinted: 1984.30; 1985.23

35 ____. "Poet in Training." *Atlantic Monthly* 249 (May): 102-5.

> Review of *The Journals*. The entries "give us . . . not the Sylvia Plath we think of as Sylvia Plath but her spiritual younger sister, a kind of Sylvia Plath in training." The material left out by the editors is more intriguing than what is included. *The Bell Jar* is a much superior example of Plath's prose.

36 RATINER, STEVEN. "New Collections Reveal Literary Development of Poets Plath and Sexton." *Christian Science Monitor*, 27 January, p. 15.

> Review of *The Collected Poems*. The arrangement of the poems in chronological order is a help to those who wish to study Plath's artistic development. The collection underscores Plath's superb craftsmanship. She was not simply a "mad genius."

37 RATNER, ROCHELLE. "Sylvia Plath: Beyond the Biographical." In *American Writing Today*. Edited by Richard Kostelanetz. Washington, D.C.: U.S. International Communication Agency, pp. 55-67.

> Attempts to separate Plath's work from the myth surrounding her. "The tortured, suicidal image has done her more harm than good." Several poems are discussed, mostly from *Ariel*. They lend support to the notion that Plath was "a Romantic poet working within the Classical tradition."

38   Review of *The Collected Poems. Choice* 19 (March): 920.
      Commends Ted Hughes on his painstaking arrangement of
Plath's poetry and on his "extensive endnotes to the mature poems." In
this volume, readers may trace Plath's "poetic vision" as well as "her
sense of the inescapably tragic."

39   Review of *The Collected Poems. Christian Science Monitor*, 3
      December, p. 14.
      Shows Plath's remarkable development over the years from
"unremarkable" work to "strong, original voice. . . ."

40   Review of *The Collected Poems. Virginia Quarterly Review* 58
      (Spring): 58.
      Praises Plath's "morbid, but exquisite sensibility." She remains
a "fine poet" despite the disservice done to her by her "personal legend
and feminist martyrology." She stands in the tradition of Poe and
Faulkner.

41   Review of *The Journals. Booklist* 78 (15 March): 922.
      The selections are "readable," and the editors have avoided
"sensationalism." Plath's development as writer and thinker can be
traced throughout.

42   Review of *The Journals. Choice* 20 (September): 87.
      Despite the deletions made by Ted Hughes, the material is
"absorbing." Plath's "enormous talent" is evident throughout.

43   Review of *The Journals. Kirkus Reviews* 50 (1 March): 329.
      The volume contains much less morbidity than readers may
expect to find. Instead, there is "an almost exhilarating sense of forward
movement, . . . an urge to love and succeed that *seems* far stronger than
[Plath's] dark, suicidal despair." Students of Plath's creative work will
find in *The Journals* a wealth of "background material."

44   Review of *The Journals. National Review* 34 (16 April): 434.

1982

> Plath's journals were "made from what the poet liked to refer
> to as her 'Sargasso.'"

45   Review of *The Journals*. *Publishers Weekly* 221 (12 March): 72.
     The material in this volume is "often verbose but seldom dull."
It exposes Plath's "struggle with her inner demons." Partially reprinted:
1983.20.

46   ROBERTS, NEIL. "Sylvia Plath Collected." *English* 31 (Spring): 73-
     79.
     Review of *The Collected Poems*. The book's important
contribution is the accurate dating of the poems. In general, however,
the "previously uncollected poems add [little of importance] to the
oeuvre."

47   SALAMONE, ANTHONY. Review of *The Journals of Sylvia Plath*.
     Best Sellers 42 (July): 144.
     Notes the difficulty readers will have taking editor Frances
McCullough's advice to "let [the] book speak for itself." Excessive
editorial cutting makes "the complete understanding of this talented but
tragic writer" impossible.

48   SANAZARO, LEONARD. "A Note on Ted Hughes' 'An Icon' and
     Sylvia Plath's 'Medallion.'" *Notes on Contemporary Literature* 12
     (May): 9-10.
     Compares the two poems and concludes that "for Hughes, the
value and immortality in art has become implicit through Plath's poem,
composed over twenty years prior to his own."

49   ____. "On the Decline of the Oracle, 1955-57: William James and
     Sylvia Plath's Dryad Poems." *Studia Mystica* 5 (Spring): 59-70.
     Explains the influence of William James's *The Varieties of
Religious Experience* on Sylvia Plath and on her work. Explicates three
of the early poems concluding that Plath came to realize that "the
modern mind had forfeited any genuine insight into spiritual reality
thus impoverishing an important aspect of human life; and women had

been denied pre-eminence in a world that had become devoid of transcendent and mystical experience."

50 SCHAEFFER, SUSAN FROMBERG. "Sylvia Plath: The Artist Possessed." *Sun-Times*, 11 April, "Show" section, p. 22.
Review of *The Journals*. Records "a remarkable woman's attempt to define herself both as an artist and as a female." The editing by Ted Hughes and Frances McCullough is "brilliant."

51 SCHREIBER, LE ANNE. Review of *The Journals of Sylvia Plath*. *New York Times*, 21 April, p. C-21.
Expresses disappointment that Ted Hughes has offered only a "very truncated and no doubt censored version" of Plath's diaries. The two questions which dominate the journals are "can a selfish, eccentric, jealous female write [anything] worthwhile? And can she mate?" One can hear Plath's "own voice" in these journals.

52 SCHWARZ, MARY. "A Cupful of Words." *National Review* 34 (February): 177-78.
Review of *The Collected Poems*. Although some of the poems are flawed "by caustic or Gothic denouements, ... " many of the "phrases and images ... are superb."

53 SMITH, DAVE. "Sylvia Plath, The Electric Horse." *American Poetry Review* 11 (January-February): 43-46.
The Collected Poems records the way poetry became Sylvia Plath's life. Her example has allowed all women poets since Plath to write successfully. Discounts all "perverse" arguments which "begin with the fact of Plath's suicide and work back to find the poems a script of illness." The manner of her death changes nothing. Lists the poets who influenced Plath. Reprinted: 1988.76.

54 STATON, SHIRLEY F., "The Great Divide: Gender in Sylvia Plath's Short Fiction." *Women and Literature* 2:206-221.
Discusses Plath's short stories as "attempts to mediate [the] antagonisms" inherent in the "power struggles [of] life against death,

1982

victor against victim, male against female." The later stories show an "equalizing" of power in the male-female struggle as more power is given to the woman. This shift is evidence of Plath's "growing insight into matriarchal power."

55 STEWART, PENNY. "Plath's Metaphors." *Explicator* 40 (Spring): 60.

The key to the "riddle" of Plath's poem "Metaphors" lies in the number *nine*, which refers to the number of lines, syllables in each line, letters in the title, and months in a full-term pregnancy.

56 STUEWE, PAUL. Review of *The Collected Poems*. *Quill and Quire* 48 (April): 33.

Recommends this edition to Plath followers for its "previously unpublished juvenalia." Praises Ted Hughes for providing a "readable text."

57 TARTT, ALISON. Review of *The Journals*. *Library Journal* 107 (15 April): 813.

Unlike *Letters Home*, *The Journals* contain "a complex and accurate record of Plath's struggle to know and express her real self." Its most important contribution is its exposure of "the development of Plath's style – from ... feminine burbling and posed cynicism to the authentic voice ... of her mature poems."

58 VAN DYNE, SUSAN R. "'More Terrible Than She Ever Was': The Manuscripts of Sylvia Plath's Bee Poems." In *Sylvia Plath, Stings, Original Drafts of the Poem in Facsimile, Reproduced from the Sylvia Plath Collection at Smith College* (Northampton, Massachusetts: Smith College Library Rare Book Room, 1982).

Examines the successive drafts of the bee poems in order to show their connection to Plath's personal life as a daughter, a mother, and a jilted wife. Comments on the significance of the drafts being written on the backs of manuscript pages from *The Bell Jar* and also on the backs of certain of Ted Hughes's poems. Concludes that "reading the published version of the bee poems against the worksheets brings to light a covert text." Reprinted: 1984.38.

1982

59   VENDLER, HELEN. "An Intractable Metal." *New Yorker* 57 (15
     February): 124-38.
         Plath's public subjects are "well-worn," but they "maintain
themselves in passion without lacking a strict, informing intelligence."
Briefly compares her to Emily Dickinson and George Herbert.
Mentions the speed with which Plath swings from one mood or tone to
another, "like a dangerously swinging needle." Reprinted: 1985.28.

60   WAGNER, LINDA W. "Plath's 'Lady Lazarus.'" *Explicator* 41 (Fall):
     50-52.
         Maintains that "Lady Lazarus" is more a poem about the
turmoil that caused Plath to consider suicide than about the actual
suicide attempt. Its themes – strained male-female relationships,
society's demand for women's conformity, men's "physical supremacy,"
sacrifices made for art's sake, the ultimate triumph of the clever, sly
woman, and the "subtle or outright disrobing, dismemberment, or death
of the female" – appear in several other late poems as well.

61   WERNER, CRAIG HANSEN. *Paradoxical Resolutions: American
     Fiction since James Joyce*. Urbana: University of Illinois Press, 1982,
     pp. 50-56.
         Sees Plath's *The Bell Jar* as being critical of Joyce's *Portrait of
the Artist as a Young Man* in that Plath "emphasizes the psychological
destructiveness of a self-absorbed rejection of reality." *The Bell Jar*
"follows *The Portrait* in its concern with the interaction of the artist and
her image within the work." Esther is Plath's Stephen Dedalus, and she
draws heavily on Joyce for thematic and structural principles.

62   WIMSATT, MARGARET. Review of the *Journals of Sylvia Plath*.
     America 147 (24-31 July): 58-59.
         Poses the question, "What blocked [Plath]? Why was she not
famous, even rich, so that that last sad chapter need not have been
written?" Readers of this book will likely supply their own very different
answers.

63   WOOD, DAVID. "Art as Transcendence in Sylvia Plath's *Ariel*."
     Kyushu American Literature 23 (May): 25-34.

1982

Explicates several *Ariel* poems in order to show that Plath's goal was to transcend her own experience through poetry. She was "exploring her own psyche through her work."

64   YOUNG, DAVID. "Poetry 1981: Review Essay." *Field: Contemporary Poetry and Poetics* 26 (Spring): 77-86.

A review essay of *The Collected Poems*. Plath's volume is compared to Anne Sexton's *The Complete Poems*, and Plath is judged to be by far the better of the two. She surpasses both Sexton and her former mentor, Robert Lowell. Plath's crowning achievement is her ability to display "verbal intensity." Her work is, like that of her true predecessors, Thomas, Lowell, and Roethke, "an intense music rising miraculously through ordinary speech. . . ." Those who portray Plath as "feminist martyr, romantic prodigy, and helpless psychotic" are mistaken. She was, instead, a "greatly gifted and deeply unhappy poet."

65   ZERBY, CHUCK. "Poet at Her Worst in Journals." *Daily Hampshire Gazette*, 28 April, p. 25.

An interview with Frances McCullough, editor of the *Journals of Sylvia Plath*, is included in the review. The question of whether or not private journals should be published at all is a legitimate one; however, Plath's journals benefit readers in two ways. First, they debunk the romantic notion of psychic pain as glamorous. Second, they expose the tenacity of an artist "to see things as they are, herself included."

66   ZIVLEY, SHERRY LUTZ. "Ted Hughes's *Apologia Pro Matrimonio Suo*." *New England Quarterly* 55 (June): 187-20.

Describes Hughes's *The Earth-Owl and Other Moon People* as his effort to speak about Sylvia Plath and his marriage to her. It chronicles both the "joys . . . and the unhappiness" of the marriage. He purposely employs many of Plath's "images and techniques" in creating this portrait of their lives together.

1983

1   BEIRNE, DANIEL J. "Plath's 'Two Campers in Cloud Country.'"
    Explicator 42 (Fall): 61-62.
        Disagrees with critics who argue that "the reference to Lethe
    [in the poem] is consistent with the suicidal preoccupation of Plath's
    other meditations. Maintains, instead, that crossing Lethe represents
    renewal and rebirth, the "benefits of vacation and the powers of sleep.
    The campers' vacation is a departure from routine duty and obligation."

2   CARTOUN, EMILIE. "Modern Mythology: Anais Nin and Sylvia
    Plath." *San Francisco Review of Books* 7 (January-February): 30-31.
        Review of *The Journals*. Compares and contrasts Plath's work
    with *The Early Diaries of Anais Nin, Volume Two, 1920-23*. They led
    similar young lives; however, Nin's ended in triumph, and Plath's, in
    tragedy.

3   CHASIN, HELEN. "What Have You Done? What Have You
    Done?" *Yale Review* 72 (Spring): 426-39.
        Review of *The Collected Poems* and *The Journals*. Plath's
    journals are more "believable" than are *Letters Home*, but both they and
    her collected poems will engender more of the misguided Plath
    criticism that has existed since her death: "Confusion of the art with the
    biography, of textual analysis with postmortems and autopsies."

4   FAAS, EKBERT. "Chapters of a Shared Mythology: Sylvia Plath
    and Ted Hughes." In *The Achievement of Ted Hughes*. Edited by
    Keith Sagar. Athens: University of Georgia Press, pp. 107-204.
        Questions other critics' assertions that Plath's desire for
    rebirth was as significant as her "sojourn on the other side of sanity and
    life." Despite her stated determination to write "the strongest female
    paean yet for the creative forces of nature" what she consistently
    produced were "poems of a more sinister nature." Presents an analysis
    of both Plath's and Hughes's poems, pointing out how and where they
    drew from each other's work.

1983

5   GILBERT, SANDRA M. "Teaching 'Daddy' to Speak to Under-
graduates." *Bulletin of the Association of Departments of English* 76
(Winter): 38-42.
    Offers suggestions for teaching Plath's "Daddy" to under-
graduates. Plath's intriguing life and death have transformed her "into a
sort of literary version of Marilyn Monroe," a fact which causes many
students and teachers alike to approach her work as strictly
autobiographical. Suggestions for avoiding such pitfalls are presented.

6   HAWTHORN, JEREMY. "The Bell Jar and the Larger Things:
Sylvia Plath." In *Multiple Personality and the Disintegration of Literary
Character from Oliver Goldsmith to Sylvia Plath*. New York: St.
Martin's Press, pp. 117-34.
    Explains Esther Greenwood's breakdown in *The Bell Jar* as a
"personality dissociation" resulting from the "dilemma ... of a woman
not granted the luxury of a double life." Women may be offered several
choices but only one choice may be made, and each choice offered is
"inadequate and unsatisfying" in itself. Also explores the connections
between the concerns and images in *The Bell Jar* and those in the
poetry.

7   HUF, LINDA. "*The Bell Jar* (1963): The Apprenticeship of Sylvia
Plath." In *A Portrait of the Artist as a Young Woman: The Writer as
Heroine in American Literature*. New York: Frederick Unger, pp.
125-47.
    Presents a plot analysis of *The Bell Jar* in order to prove that
Plath critics who maintain the artist was "'bitchy,'" "'spiteful,'" and
"'mean'" are wrong. Those who dismiss Plath as "'hysterical, morbid,
and perverse,'" and who use her suicide to support this opinion, only
exhibit their total lack of a legitimate explanation for Plath's "inordinate
rage." The real reason for the disintegration of the heroine is that she is
suffocating inside the bell jar of patriarchal society, which insists upon
"traditional feminine interests and abilities." Esther Greenwood lacks
such interests and thus is made to feel like a monster.

8   HUGHES, TED. "Sylvia Plath and Her Journals." *Grand Street* 1
(Spring): 86-99.

Explains the development of Plath's poetry in terms of death, birth, and rebirth. Points to "The Stones" as the poem which represents a crucial turning point in Plath's work. "It is unlike anything that had gone before . . . and throughout the poem what we hear coming clear is the now familiar voice of *Ariel*." A much shorter version of this same essay was published as the forward to *The Journals of Sylvia Plath*. Reprinted: 1985.12.

9   KAUL, FREDERICK R. *American Fictions, 1940-1980*. New York: Harper and Row, pp. 140-41.

Plath's *The Bell Jar* resembles Salinger's *The Catcher in the Rye* because of 'their ability to juxtapose highs and lows in rapid succession." *The Bell Jar* is a relative failure since it "reaches for significances Plath is unable to deliver on." She is a better poet than novelist because she can sustain intensity only in "short bursts," not over the "longer haul."

10   KOLICH, AUGUSTUS M. "Does Fiction Have to Be Made Better than Life?" *Modern Fiction Studies* 29 (Summer): 170-74.

Maintains that *The Bell Jar* is too intimately connected with Plath's autobiography to be a literary or "imaginative" success: "As long as Plath's work remains transparently open to the riveting stare of biographical voyeurism, it can never be . . . fictional." Much of this "voyeurism" can be blamed on critics and editors of her work.

11   KUMAR, SUKRITA PAUL. "Sylvia Plath: A Self in 'Halflighted Castles.'" In *Existentialism in American Literature*. Edited by Ruby Chatterji. Atlantic Highlands, N. J.: Humanities Press, pp. 71-79.

Explores the various "selves" Plath became as shown in several of her poems. "Instead of making her soar high in release, the hallucinatory projectings of her self reduce her ego to a numbness."

12   LARKIN, PHILIP. "Horror Poet." In *Required Writing: Miscellaneous Pieces, 1955-1982*. London: Faber and Faber, pp. 278-81.

Reprint of 1982.23. Published in 1984 by Farrar, Straus and Giroux, New York.

1983

13   LEVINE, MIRIAM. "*The Journals of Sylvia Plath.*" *American Book Review* (May-June): 3-4.

   Analyzes the Plath *Journals* as a record "in which the writer's work-life and search for identity are almost indistinguishable." Probes Plath's dual nature as essentially a "split between mind and body." Concludes by pointing out the typically American tendency of critics to focus on how "self-destructive writers could have saved themselves." Suggests that for Plath, perhaps salvation was not possible. Reprinted: 1988.52.

14   MARTONE, JOHN. Review of *The Journals*. *World Literature Today* 57 (Spring): 295.

   Speculates that Plath's journals "may be the most powerful record we have of the struggle to be human in our time." They certainly represent Plath's best prose writing despite the "controversial" editorial cuts.

15   MILLER, ALICE. "Sylvia Plath: An Example of Forbidden Suffering." In *For Your Own Good: Hidden Cruelty in Childrearing and the Roots of Violence*. New York: Farrar, Straus and Giroux, pp. 254-60.

   Maintains that the violence and rage in Plath's work is a result of Plath's being forbidden, as a child, "to experience and articulate . . . suffering, the pain felt at being wounded." These repressed emotions intensified "until adulthood, when they [were] finally discharged, but not on the object that caused them."

16   MORRIS, CHRISTOPHER. "Order and Chaos in Plath's 'The Colossus.'" *Concerning Poetry* 15 (Fall): 33-42.

   Reviews past critical views of "The Colossus" as limited. Traditionally it has been seen as its persona's "effort to understand existence by recollecting her father." However, its true importance is in its expression of "the speaker's inability to ever find, through poetry, a clear understanding of her position."

17   OSTRIKER, ALICIA. "The Americanization of Sylvia." In *Writing Like a Woman*. Ann Arbor: University of Michigan Press, pp. 42-58. Reprint of 1968.B10*. Reprinted: 1984.28.

18   "Publication of Drafts by Sylvia Plath Marks Opening of Collection at Smith College." *Daily Hampshire Gazette*, 12 January, p. 24.
        Cites the opening of the Smith College Collection of "4000 pages of [Plath's] manuscripts and typescripts, including more than 200 poems in successive drafts, among them 'Stings' and 850 pages of unpublished journals."

19   Review of *The Journals*. *New York Times Book Review*, 4 August, p. 27.
        Shows Plath to be "relentless in her dedication to her craft." The editorial omissions make this volume a "peculiarly broken record."

20   Review of *The Journals*. *Publishers Weekly* 223 (24 June): 56.
        This review of the paperback edition is an abbreviated reprint of 1982.45.

21   ROSENTHAL, M. L., and GALL, SALLY M. "'Pure? What Does It Mean?' Notes on Sylvia Plath's Poetic Art." *American Poetry Review* 7 (May-June): 37-40.
        Discusses Plath's ability "to write at a pitch of pure intensity" without losing control of her art. Also stresses the aesthetic distance she maintains. Analyzes "Hardcastle Crags," "The Other," "Fever 103," and comments on the chronology of the poems in *Ariel*.

22   SANAZARO, LEONARD. "Plath's 'Lady Lazarus.'" *Explicator* 41 (Spring): 54-57.
        Traces Plath's interest in the Lazarus story back to her undergraduate days at Smith College.

23   ___. "The Transfiguring Self: Sylvia Plath, a Reconsideration." *Centennial Review* 27 (Winter): 62-74.
        Employs biographical material and careful textual scrutiny to illuminate the "universal themes that run throughout Plath's *oeuvre*." Both her "advocates and [her] detractors" miss the mark because they "fail ... to treat the emotional and intellectual complexities of the poems themselves." Much Plath criticism falls into one of two extremes:

1983

"Either the poems are thoroughly immersed in the poet's biography and rendered incapable of independent existence as works of art; or they are defensively divorced from the poet's life . . . , thus denuding them of the important personal and world milieu in which they came into being." Reprinted: 1984.34.

24   VAN DYNE, SUSAN. "Fueling the Phoenix Fire: The Manuscripts of Sylvia Plath's Lady Lazarus.'" *Massachusetts Review* 24 (Summer): 395-410.
       Analyzes the Plath's deletions and revisions of "Lady Lazarus" and comments on their significance. Points out that Plath's penchant for using the backs of her earlier manuscripts was significant in that often the new work in some way paralleled the old. Her "Lady Lazarus" worksheets show the "stages in the reconstruction of the heroine, and her separation from the male antagonist." Plath was attempting "to resurrect an image of a powerful, autonomous heroine [while at the same time attempting] to reduce to ashes any remnant of a self derivatively defined by her relationship to [Ted] Hughes.

25   WAGNER, LINDA W. "Sylvia Plath's *Journals*." *Contemporary Literature* 24 (Winter): 521-23.
       The tone of Plath's journal entries runs the gamut from "euphoric" to "strained" and depressed. Some entries show "genuine" joy in her marriage, while others "show the rivalry [she] felt, the inferiority. . . ." The book benefits Plath scholars who look for connections between her diary and her poetry and prose. Thus Hughes's destruction of some of this "valuable literary material . . . saddens us all." Reprinted: 1988.86 as "*The Journals of Sylvia Plath*."

26   WILLIAMSON, ALAN. "Confession and Tragedy." *Poetry* 142 (June): 170-78 passim.
       Reviews Plath's *The Collected Poems* and Sexton's *The Complete Poems*. Maintains that Plath was more gifted than Sexton. Calls "confessional poetry" a "tragic poetry, because it deals with the struggle and failure to escape, not only from the individual personality . . . , but from what are felt to be the limitations of human nature itself." Examines several of Plath's poems and comments on the "peculiarly complicated" publication history of her work.

27 "X-Ray View of a Struggling Poet." *Christian Science Monitor*, 2 September, p. 8.
    Review of *The Journals*. Records her effort to maintain emotional stability. Offers those readers "unwilling to puzzle out her many difficult poems" easier access to Plath.

1984

1 ANNAS, PAMELA J. "The Self in the World: The Social Context of Sylvia Plath's Late Poems." In *Critical Essays on Sylvia Plath*. Edited by Linda W. Wagner. Boston: G. K. Hall & Co., pp. 130-39.
    Reprint of 1980.1.

2 BERE, CAROL. *"Letters Home: Correspondence, 1950-1963."* In *Critical Essays on Sylvia Plath*. Edited by Linda W. Wagner. Boston: G. K. Hall & Co., pp. 59-62.
    Reprint of 1977.3. Reprinted: 1988.8.

3 BOLLOBAS, ENIKO. "Woman *and* Poet? Conflicts in the Poetry of Emily Dickinson, Sylvia Plath, and Anne Sexton." In *The Origins and Originality of American Culture*. Budapest: Akademiai Kiado, pp. 375-83 passim.
    Compares the three poets to one another in terms of their common dilemma: "whether to perfect one's life or art." The choice is more problematic if the artist is a woman. "If she succeeds as a poet, she will fail as a woman, or vice versa."

4 BRANS, JO. "The Girl Who Wanted to Be God." In *Critical Essays on Sylvia Plath*. Edited by Linda W. Wagner. Boston: G. K. Hall & Co., pp. 56-59.
    Reprint of 1976.8. Reprinted: 1988.11.

5 BROWNSTONE, ALAN. "Awesome Fragments." In *Critical Essays on Sylvia Plath*. Edited by Linda W. Wagner. Boston: G. K. Hall & Co., pp. 55-56.
    Reprint of 1971.B14* (under the name *Brownjohn*).

1984

6   BUELL, FREDERICK. "Sylvia Plath's Traditionalism." In *Critical Essays on Sylvia Plath*. Edited by Linda W. Wagner. Boston: G. K. Hall & Co., pp. 140-54.
    Reprint of 1976.10.

7   CALIO, LOUISE. "A Rebirth of the Goddess in Contemporary Women Poets of the Spirit." *Studia Mystica* 7 (Spring): 50-9.
    Characterizes Plath and Anne Sexton as "pioneers in the journey into feminine consciousness." In *Ariel*, Plath presents the Goddess "in her destructive aspect." Her search for the Goddess within herself is impeded by the "false gods" of "daddy, husband, children and even other women. . . ." In *Ariel* she finally experiences transformation and is given "a voice powerful enough to . . . overcome 'daddy.'"

8   COYLE, SUSAN. "Images of Madness and Retrieval: An Exploration of Metaphor in *The Bell Jar*." *Studies in American Fiction* 12 (Autumn): 161-74.
    Examines Plath's metaphors "of death, of alienation, of losing one's self and, later, regaining that self. Applies Annis Pratt's assertions in *Archetypal Patterns in Women's Fiction* to *The Bell Jar* and discusses Esther Greenwood's "alienation from [both written and verbal] language" at length.

9   DAVISON, PETER. "Inhabited by a Cry: The Last Poetry of Sylvia Plath." In *Critical Essays on Sylvia Plath*. Edited by Linda W. Wagner. Boston: G. K. Hall & Co., pp. 38-41.
    Reprint of 1966.B5*. Reprinted: 1988.17.

10 DICKIE, MARGARET. "Sylvia Plath's Narrative Strategies." In *Critical Essays on Sylvia Plath*. Edited by Linda W. Wagner. Boston: G. K. Hall & Co., pp. 170-82.
    Reprint of 1982.10.

11 DRAKE, BARBARA. "Perfection Is Terrible; It Cannot Have Children . . . " In *Critical Essays on Sylvia Plath*. Edited by Linda

W. Wagner. Boston: G. K. Hall & Co., pp. 42-43.
Reprint of 1967.B5*.

12 DUNN, DOUGLAS. "Damaged Instruments." In *Critical Essays on Sylvia Plath*. Edited by Linda W. Wagner. Boston: G. K. Hall & Co., pp. 51-53.
Reprint of 1971.B19*. Reprinted: 1988.21.

13 DYSON, A. E. Review of *The Colossus*. In *Critical Essays on Sylvia Plath*. Edited by Linda W. Wagner. Boston: G. K. Hall & Co., pp. 27-30.
Reprint of 1961.B2*. Reprinted: 1988.22.

14 GILBERT, SANDRA M. "In Yeats' House: The Death and Resurrection of Sylvia Plath." In *Critical Essays on Sylvia Plath*. Edited by Linda W. Wagner. Boston: G. K. Hall & Co., pp. 204-22.
Plath expressed "loyalty to the male tradition" to which she felt she belonged. At the same time she "hinted at her feelings of rivalry toward these men." Examines "the implications of . . . [Plath's] self-definition, rising, as it did, out of divided loyalties, ambivalences, ambiguities." Surveys both the male and the female writers Plath thought of as her "masters."

15 GRANT, DAMIAN. "*Winter Trees.*" In *Critical Essays on Sylvia Plath*. Edited by Linda W. Wagner. Boston: G. K. Hall & Co., pp. 53-55.
Reprint of 1972.B9*. Reprinted: 1988.29.

16 HANKOFF, L. D. "Poetry, Adolescence, and Suicide." *Pharos* 47 (Spring): 7-12.
Examines the suicide impulses of three artists. Concludes that the "creative act" is not therapeutic. Artistic "self-expression" may, in fact, have "negative effects . . . at critical periods" for those in whom "a psychopathological state of mind prevails."

1984

17 HARRIS, MASON. "*The Bell Jar.*" In *Critical Essays on Sylvia Plath*.
    Edited by Linda W. Wagner. Boston: G. K. Hall & Co., pp. 34-38.
    Reprint of 1973.12. Reprinted: 1988.31.

18 HILL, DOUGLAS. "Living and Dying." In *Critical Essays on Sylvia
    Plath*. Edited by Linda W. Wagner. Boston: G. K. Hall & Co., pp.
    62-64.
    Reprint of 1978.8. Reprinted: 1988.32.

19 JAIDKA, MANJU. "Sentimental Violence: A Note on Diane
    Wakoski and Sylvia Plath." *Notes on Contemporary Literature* 14
    (November): 2.
        Notes the similarities between Wakoski's "Dancing on the
    Grave of a Son of a Bitch" and Plath's "Daddy." Both are ritual[s] of
    exorcism" performed to free the female personae from the male
    "masters" who oppress them.

20 KIRKHAM, MICHAEL. "Sylvia Plath." *Queen's Quarterly* 91
    (Spring): 153-66.
        The Collected Poems of Sylvia Plath provides "at last a clear
    view of the emergence ... of her themes." Includes a thorough
    explication of several poems which confirm that Plath was not, as many
    critics have suggested, a confessional poet. Instead of "lack of control,"
    the poems "sometimes show too much or the wrong kind of control. . . .
    [Plath's] method of ... distancing personal emotion ... must be
    reassessed." Reprinted: 1988.43.

21 LERNER, LAURENCE. "Sylvia Plath." In *Critical Essays on Sylvia
    Plath*. Edited by Linda W. Wagner. Boston: G. K. Hall & Co., pp.
    64-67.
    Reprint of 1982.24. Reprinted: 1988.50.

22 LIBBY, ANTHONY. "Sylvia Plath, God's Lioness and the Priest of
    Sycorox." In *Mythologies of Nothing: Mystical Death in American*

Poetry, 1940-70. Urbana and Chicago: University of Illinois Press, pp. 126-52.
    Reprint of 1974.12.

23   MAZZENTI, ROBERT. "Plath in Italy." In *Critical Essays on Sylvia Plath*. Edited by Linda W. Wagner. Boston: G. K. Hall & Co., pp. 193-204.
    Includes a brief chronology of the publication of Italian translations of Plath, as well as a survey of the critical responses these works received in Italy from 1969 to 1983.

24   MILFORD, NANCY. "*The Journals of Sylvia Plath*." In *Critical Essays on Sylvia Plath*. Edited by Linda W. Wagner. Boston: G. K. Hall & Co., pp. 77-81.
    Reprint of 1982.29.

25   MURDOCH, BRIAN. "Transformations of the Holocaust: Auschwitz in Modern Lyric Poetry." *Comparative Literature Studies* 11 (June): 123-50.
    Sylvia Plath was far from the first poet to use holocaust imagery in her work. However, her use of it on a personal level is unique and raises the question by George Steiner, "Do any of us have license to locate our personal disasters, raw as these may be, in Auschwitz?" The answer is that "Sylvia Plath's use of this imagery, even if it cannot perhaps be justified," can at least be explained. Traces the roots of "death-camp imagery" back to the work of poets "who were involved with the events" at the time they were occurring. Sylvia Plath "represents a final stage of development of the Auschwitz imagery."

26   MYERS, E. LUCAS. "The Tranquilized Fifties." In *Critical Essays on Sylvia Plath*. Edited by Linda W. Wagner. Boston: G. K. Hall & Co., pp. 30-32.
    Reprint of 1962.B5*. Reprinted: 1988.58.

27   NANCE, GUINEVARA A., and JONES, JUDITH P. "Doing away with Daddy: Exorcism and Sympathetic Magic in Plath's Poetry." In

1984

> *Critical Essays on Sylvia Plath*. Edited by Linda W. Wagner. Boston:
> G. K. Hall & Co., pp. 124-30.
> Reprint of 1978.20.

28   OSTRIKER, ALICIA. "The Americanization of Sylvia." In *Critical
     Essays on Sylvia Plath*. Edited by Linda W. Wagner. Boston: G. K.
     Hall & Co., pp. 97-109.
     Reprint of 1968.B10*; 1983.17.

29   PERLOFF, MARJORIE. "Angst and Animism in the Poetry of
     Sylvia Plath." In *Critical Essays on Sylvia Plath*. Edited by Linda W.
     Wagner. Boston: G. K. Hall & Co., pp. 109-124.
     Reprint of 1970.B10*.

30   POLLITT, KATHA. "A Note of Triumph." In *Critical Essays on
     Sylvia Plath*. Edited by Linda W. Wagner. Boston: G. K. Hall & Co.,
     pp. 67-72.
     Reprint of 1972.34. Reprinted: 1985.23.

31   PORTER, PETER. "Collecting Her Strength." In *Critical Essays on
     Sylvia Plath*. Edited by Linda W. Wagner. Boston: G. K. Hall & Co.,
     pp. 46-47.
     Reprint of 1971.B48*. Reprinted: 1988.64

32   PRITCHARD, WILLIAM H. "An Interesting Minor Poet?" In *Criti-
     cal Essays on Sylvia Plath*. Edited by Linda W. Wagner. Boston: G.
     K. Hall & Co., pp. 72-77.
     Reprint of 1981.18. Reprinted: 1988.66.

33   ROSENTHAL, M. L. "Metamorphosis of a Book (*The Colossus*)."
     In *Critical Essays on Sylvia Plath*. Edited by Linda W. Wagner.
     Boston: G. K. Hall & Co., pp. 32-34.
     Reprint of 1967.B10*. Reprinted: 1988.67.

1984

34   SANAZARO, LEONARD. "The Transfiguring Self: Sylvia Plath, a Reconsideration." In *Critical Essays on Sylvia Plath*. Edited by Linda W. Wagner. Boston: G. K. Hall & Co., pp. 87-97.
     Reprint of 1983.23.

35   SCHWARTZ, YALE. "Binary Features in the Semantic of Literary Texts: The Case of Represented Sensory Properties." In *Quaderni di semantica: Rivista internaziorale di semantica teorica e applicata/An International Journal of Theoretical and Applied Semantics* 9 (June): 206-15.
     Discusses Plath's "Tulips" as one example of "binary structuring." In the poem "the psychophysical state of the 'I'" corresponds to certain "properties" within the text, while "the awakening 'life-force' in the 'I'" corresponds to others. Although the two sets of properties are not opposites, "each property is perceived as the equivalent of any other property in its own [set]."

36   SEED, DAVID. Review of *The Collected Poems*. *Études anglaise*s 37 (January-March): 108.
     Commends Ted Hughes for finally "conflat[ing] [the earlier] volumes . . . to produce what will surely be the definitive edition of . . . Plath's poetry." Any serious Plath student will find the book "indispensable."

37   STILWELL, ROBERT L. Review of *Ariel*. In *Critical Essays on Sylvia Plath*. Edited by Linda W. Wagner. Boston: G. K. Hall & Co., pp. 44-45.
     Partial reprint of 1968.B11*.

38   VAN DYNE, SUSAN R. "'More Terrible Than She Ever Was': The Manuscripts of Sylvia Plath's Bee Poems." In *Critical Essays on Sylvia Plath*. Edited by Linda W. Wagner. Boston: G. K. Hall & Co., pp. 154-70.
     Reprint of 1982.58.

1984

39 WAGNER, LINDA W. Introduction to *Critical Essays on Sylvia Plath*. Edited by Linda C. Wagner. Boston: G. K. Hall & Co., pp. 1-24.

An overview of twenty years of Plath criticism. Explains the two basic types of Plath critics–the "structuralist, mythic linguistic" variety and "those . . . who employ the confessional, art-equated-with-madness perspective." Several critics are quoted extensively, most of whom are poets themselves. "Regardless of gender, race, or position, fellow poets have been the chief supporters of Plath's work."

40 ____, ed. *Critical Essays on Sylvia Plath*. Boston: G. K. Hall & Co., 231 pp.

Contents: A. E. Dyson's Review of *The Colossus*; E. Lucas Myers's "The Tranquilized Fifties"; M. L. Rosenthal's "Metamorphosis of a Book (*The Colossus*)"; Mason Harris's "*The Bell Jar*"; Peter Davison's "Inhabited by a Cry: The Last Poetry of Sylvia Plath"; Barbara Drake's "'Perfection Is Terrible; It Cannot Have Children . . . '"; Robert L. Stilwell's Review of *Ariel*; Peter Porter's "Collecting Her Strength"; Paul West's "*Crossing the Water*"; Douglas Dunn's "Damaged Instruments"; Damian Grant's "*Water Trees*"; Alan Brownstone's "Awesome Fragments"; Jo Brans's "The Girl Who Wanted to Be God"; Carol Bere's "*Letters Home: Correspondence 1950-1963*"; Douglas Hill's "Living and Dying"; Laurence Lerner's "Sylvia Plath"; Katha Pollitt's "A Note of Triumph"; William H. Pritchard's "An Interesting Minor Poet?"; Nancy Milford's "The Journals of Sylvia Plath"; Leonard Sanazaro's "The Transfiguing Self: Sylvia Plath"; Alicia Ostriker's "The Americanization of Sylvia"; Marjorie Perloff's "Angst and Animism in the Poetry of Sylvia Plath"; Guinevara A. Nance and Judith P. Jones's "Doing Away with Daddy: Exorcisim and Sympathetic Magic in Plath's Poetry"; Pamela J. Annas's "The Self in the World: The Social Context of Sylvia Plath's Late Poems"; Frederick Buell's "Sylvia Plath's Traditionalism"; Susan R. Van Dyne's "'More Terrible Than She Ever Was': The Manuscripts of Sylvia Plath's Bee Poems"; Margaret Dickie's "Sylvia Plath's Narrative Strategies"; Melody Zajdel's "Apprenticed in a Bible of Dreams: Sylvia Plath's Short Stories"; Roberta Mazzenti's "Plath in Italy"; Sandra M. Gilbert's "In Yeats' House: The Death and Resurrection of Sylvia Plath."

41 ___. "Plath's 'Ladies Home Journal' Syndrome." *Journal of American Culture* 7 (Spring-Summer): 32-38.

Explores the influences of the 1950's women's magazines and advice columns on Plath. They reinforce the conflict she was already experiencing as a senior in high school when she was writing "stories about the conflicts of career and marriage." Yet, Plath achieved at least a partial triumph. She became a writer in spite of cultural pressure to "take shorthand, . . . [d]o anything but go the way you are drawn." The contradiction between the drive to be a conventional woman writing for women's magazines and the desire to become a "great writer is enough to have driven any mid-century woman to madness."

42 WEST, PAUL. "*Crossing the Water*." In *Critical Essays on Sylvia Plath*. Edited by Linda W. Wagner. Boston: G. K. Hall & Co., pp. 48-51.

Reprint of A1972.33. See Appendix. Reprinted: 1988.90

43 WILLIAMSON, ALAN. "Real and Numinous Selves: A Reading of Sylvia Plath." In *Introspection and Contemporary Poetry*. Cambridge: Harvard University Press, pp. 26-64.

Applies the principles of Jung, Laing, and Binsivanger both to Plath and to her work. Explores the psychological significance of Plath's "Freudian self-analysis," "the immense impact" of her father's death, her mother's "tightly controlled response," Plath's own "failed marriage," and her "constant and finally overmastering, fascination with death."

44 WOOD, DAVID. "Everything You Wanted to Know about Suicide." *Kyushu American Literature* 25 (July): 7-17.

Presents a reading of *The Bell Jar* as a novel that is valuable not as an autobiographical account but "as a *poetic* statement of one individual's struggle for release from the pressures imposed on her by society." The novel's success lies in the creation of a narrator who is distant enough from Plath to tell Esther Greenwood's story at "a high degree of artistic mastery."

1984

45 ZAJDEL, MELODY. "Apprenticed in a Bible of Dreams: Sylvia Plath's Short Stories." In *Critical Essays on Sylvia Plath*. Edited by Linda W. Wagner. Boston: G. K. Hall & Co., pp. 182-93.

Establishes correspondences between several of the short stories in *Johnny Panic and the Bible of Dreams* and her subsequent novel, *The Bell Jar*. The stories are a "direct movement into [Plath's] writing of *The Bell Jar* and exhibit her preoccupation with the same themes as those found in the novel. The short stories served as her 'apprenticeship," without which she could not have achieved the "powerful craftsmanship" of *The Bell Jar*. Reprinted: 1988.93.

1985

1 ALEXANDER, PAUL. Introduction to *Ariel Ascending: Writings about Sylvia Plath*. New York: Harper and Row, pp. ix-xv.

Presents an overview of the order in which Plath's work has been published. Maintains that the goal of this collection of essays is to answer the question, "how good is [Plath's] work and will it last?" Expresses the intention of the editor to include "essays which avoid sensationalizing [the poet's] life and death and instead examine the craft of her poetry and prose."

2 ____, ed. *Ariel Ascending: Writings about Sylvia Plath*. New York: Harper and Row, 217 pp.

Contents: Helen Vendler's "An Intractable Metal"; Stanley Plumly's "What Ceremony of Words"; Joyce Carol Oates's "The Death Throes of Romanticism"; John Frederick Nims's "The Poetry of Sylvia Plath"; Barbara Hardy's "Enlargement or Derangement?"; Mary Lynn Broe's "Enigmatical, Shifting My Clarities"; Katha Pollitt's "A Note of Triumph"; Elizabeth Hardwick's "On Sylvia Plath"; Rosellen Brown's "Keeping the Self at Bay"; Howard Moss's "Dying: An Introduction"; Robert Scholes's "Esther Came Back Like A Retreaded Tire"; Vance Bourjaily's "Victoria Lucas and Elly Higgenbottom"; Ted Hughes's "Sylvia Plath and Her Journal"; Grace Sculman's "Sylvia Plath and Yaddo"; Anne Sexton's "The Barfly Ought to Sing"; A. Alvarez's "Sylvia Plath: A Memoir"; Aurelia S. Plath's "Letter Written in the Actuality of Spring."

1985

3   ALVAREZ, A. "Sylvia Plath: The Road to Suicide." In *Ariel Ascending: Writings about Sylvia Plath*. Edited by Paul Alexander. New York: Harper and Row, pp. 185-213.
        Partially published in 1971.B4*. First published in full in 1971.B7*, "Sylvia Plath: A Memoir." Condensed and published under the second title in 1971.B3* and again in 1971.B8*.

4   AXELROD, STEVEN GOULD. "The Mirror and the Shadow: Plath's Poetics of Self-Doubt." *Contemporary Literature* 26 (Fall): 286-301.
        Traces Plath's interest in mirrors and shadows back to the research she did for her honor's thesis, which was a study of "the double" in Dostoevski. Most influential were James Frazer, Otto Rank, and Sigmund Freud, and the impact of each on Plath's work is discussed in detail. Throughout her later poetry, Plath tried to reveal a "creative . . . self hidden within her" by shedding the exterior self to reveal "an inner 'queen.'" Although she succeeded at times, more often she concentrated on her fears of failure. She represented these fears with the mirror and the shadow. The former "reflect[ed] an ugly outer being but no inner queen;" the latter represented "the insubstantiality of creative nonbeing." Thus, both are symbols of Plath's own "negative vision of herself and her world."

5   ___. "The Second Destruction of Sylvia Plath." *American Poetry Review*, 14 (March-April): 17-18.
        Castigates Ted Hughes for destroying Plath's last journal entries and for heavily editing the surviving ones for publication. Suggests that Hughes's explanation for his action is "disingenuous" and that the real explanation is that Plath's last entries contained "a portrait of Hughes [that] . . . must have been devastating." Also discusses the disappearance of the novel Plath was working on shortly before her death, speculating that it probably disappeared for the same reasons the journals were destroyed. Reprinted: 1988.7.

6   BEDIENT, CALVIN. "Oh, Plath!" *Parnassus* 12 and 13:275-81.
        Discusses Plath's romanticism. She trusted the authority of her own feelings absolutely, regardless of their often childish natures. Her major achievements were "to reintroduce sublimity into American

111

1985

poetry, [to theatricalize and revitalize lyric poetry with an] attack of voice, mythic identifications, and vehemence of feeling and pace, and ... to raise poetry to a new ... aural definition." Plath has the imaginative power to turn ordinary objects into something dazzling and memorable, and she transforms pain into "something precious."

7   BOURJAILY, VANCE. "Victoria Lucas and Elly Higginbottom." In *Ariel Ascending: Writings about Sylvia Plath*. Edited by Paul Alexander. New York: Harper and Row, pp. 134-51.

Asserts that in *The Bell Jar* "Sylvia Plath was creating a character, not just spilling her guts." Uses several passages from the novel to support the contention that, although Plath was fictionalizing some events from her own life, *The Bell Jar* cannot rightly be considered autobiographical. In fact, "while Victoria Lucas was working with Ester Greenwood and Elly Higginbottom, Sylvia Plath was writing *Ariel*."

8   BROE, MARY LYNN. "'Enigmatical, Shifting My Clarities.'" In *Ariel Ascending: Writings about Sylvia Plath*. Edited by Paul Alexander. New York: Harper and Row, pp. 80-91.

A reading of Plath's poetry as evidence of Plath's powerful voice, one which "succeeds in encompassing – not negating – vital contradictions." Plath gives voice to "that complex process of interplay between the history a woman inherits and the clear articulation of her developing consciousness."

9   BROWN, ROSELLEN. "Keeping the Self at Bay." In *Ariel Ascending: Writings about Sylvia Plath*. Edited by Paul Alexander. New York: Harper and Row, pp. 116-24.

Maintains that "for Plath ... fiction served the world's purposes and poetry served the self's." As Plath became progressively more self-obsessed, then, the more time she devoted to poetry. By the end of her life, she was "all self."

10   HARDWICK, ELIZABETH. "On Sylvia Plath." In *Ariel Ascending: Writings about Sylvia Plath*. Edited by Paul Alexander. New York:

Harper and Row, pp. 100-115.
Reprint of 1971.B21*. Reprinted: 1973.11; 1974.7.

11 HARDY, BARBARA. "Enlargement or Derangement?" In *Ariel
Ascending: Writings about Sylvia Plath*. Edited by Paul Alexander.
New York: Harper and Row, pp. 61-79.
Reprint of 1970.B3*.

12 HUGHES, TED. "Sylvia Plath and Her Journals." In *Ariel
Ascending: Writings about Sylvia Plath*. Edited by Paul Alexander.
New York: Harper and Row, pp. 152-64.
Reprint of 1983.8.

13 LEHRER, SYLVIA. *The Dialectics of Art and Life: A Portrait of
Sylvia Plath as Woman and Poet*. Salzberg, Austria: Institut für
Anglistic und Amerikanistik Universität Salzburg, 22 pp.
Focuses on the interrelationship of Plath's life and poetry.
Maintains that her art influenced her life as much as her life influenced
her art. Personal experiences also served merely to spark her poetry;
therefore, she cannot be called a strictly confessional poet. Begins with
a critique of Plath criticism, then proceeds to analyze the poet and her
work based on "what is known about the chronology of her life and art."

14 LEIBOWITZ, HERBERT. "Diving and Climbing." *Parnassus* 12 and
13:6-16.
Compares and contrasts Plath's work with that of Adrienne
Rich. They are two among many women poets who, after the Civil
Rights and the Women's Movement, began to question their domestic
roles and challenged tradition. They are "emblems" of women's
changed relationship to their art. Analyzes Plath's poetry to support the
contention that she toppled tradition and "subvert[ed] pieties" by
"div[ing] into her psyche ... and prob[ing] her wounds with ...
merciless clarity." Trusting her imagination absolutely, Plath makes
theatre out of the ordinary and "rewrit[es] the rules of prosody."

1985

15 LUPTON, MARY JANE. "Women Writers and Death by Drowning." In *Amid Visions and Revisions*. Edited by Burney J. Hollis. Baltimore: Morgan State University Press, pp. 95-101 passim.

Explores the "psychological and feminist meanings of water-death, [especially the] loss of ego, defiance, baptism, eroticism, consciousness, and rebirth," using Sylvia Plath as one example. Points out that the recurring "motif" of suicide in Plath's work often is "described in terms of drowning" even when the attempts at self-destruction do not actually involve water. Kate Chopin and George Elliot are also discussed.

16 MARKEY, JANICE. "Sylvia Plath: 'The Heart Has Not Stopped.'" In *A New Tradition?: The Poetry of Sylvia Plath, Anne Sexton, and Adrienne Rich*. New York: Peter Lang, pp. 19-100.

Maintains that the biological approach to Plath's work is inadequate, largely because it too often places undue emphasis on Plath's suicide. Uses Edward Butscher, A. Alvarez, and David Holbrook as examples of this distortion. Viewing Plath as "just another member of the Confessional School" is equally inadequate. Offers, instead, a discussion of two major themes in Plath's poetry: the problem of personal relationships and "life in . . . a distorted society." Concludes by commenting on Plath's quest "for a healthy balance between her life and her work" and her commitment to "the act of writing" itself, which was therapeutic because it "helped her to cope."

17 MOSS, HOWARD. "Dying: An Introduction." In *Ariel Ascending: Writings about Sylvia Plath*. Edited by Paul Alexander. New York: Harper and Row, pp. 125-29.

Reprint of 1971.B41*; 1981.13.

18 NIMS, JOHN FREDERICK. "The Poetry of Sylvia Plath: A Technical Analysis." In *Ariel Ascending: Writings about Sylvia Plath*. Edited by Paul Alexander. New York: Harper and Row, pp. 46-60.

Reprint of 1970.B9*.

19 OATES, JOYCE CAROL. "The Death Throes of Romanticism: The Poetry of Sylvia Plath." In *Ariel Ascending: Writings about Sylvia*

1985

Plath. Edited by Paul Alexander. New York: Harper and Row, pp. 26-45.
>Reprint of 1973.B11*. Reprinted: 1974.17; 1974.18; 1977.34.

20   PERLOFF, MARJORIE. "Icon of the Fifties." *Parnassus* 12 and 13:282-85.
>Although Plath "energetically rejected" feminist views in her letters home, she was a feminist beneath the surface. The conventional life she desired – "the 'good' marriage, the babies, the ... baking of endless blueberry pies" – failed her, but it is her recounting of this life which "gives her poetry its special poignancy." Her voice can still be heard in the verse of contemporary women writers.

21   PLATH, AURELIA SCHOBER. "Letter Written in the Actuality of Spring." In *Ariel Ascending: Writings about Sylvia Plath*. Edited by Paul Alexander. New York: Harper and Row, pp. 214-17.
>Written especially for this essay collection, this letter contains, for the most part, Aurelia Plath's emphasis upon her daughter's "tendency to fuse characters and manipulate events to achieve her own artistic ends," a practice which Mrs. Plath believes, results in "cruel and false caricatures."

22   PLUMLY, STANLEY. "What Ceremony of Words." In *Ariel Ascending: Writings about Sylvia Plath*. Edited by Paul Alexander. New York: Harper and Row, pp. 13-25.
>Shows Plath to be a poet committed to 'invent[ing] form." Though *Ariel* is often "worshipped for its perceived confessional content," the poems in that volume show that Plath was still "inventing, contriving, conjuring" new forms. The predominant mode of *Ariel* is couplets and triplets, ... the short line, stanzas of psychological shorthand, of the quick take, the hook."

23   POLLITT, KATHA. "A Note of Triumph." In *Ariel Ascending: Writings about Sylvia Plath*. Edited by Paul Alexander. New York: Harper and Row, pp. 94-99.
>Reprint of 1982.34. Reprinted: 1984.30.

1985

24   SCHOLES, ROBERT. "Esther Came Back Like a Retreaded Tire."
       In *Ariel Ascending: Writings about Sylvia Plath*. Edited by Paul
       Alexander. New York: Harper and Row, pp. 130-33.
            Reprint of 1971.B53*.

25   SCHULMAN, GRACE. "Sylvia Plath and Yaddo." In *Ariel Ascend-
       ing: Writings about Sylvia Plath*. Edited by Paul Alexander. New
       York: Harper and Row, pp. 165-77.
            Traces the imagery in many of Plath's poems back to Yaddo,
       the artists' colony in New York where Plath and Ted Hughes spent two
       months in late 1959. Sees "The Colossus" as "a turning point in [Plath's]
       poems about the father, . . . the gods in her mythology, and about . . .
       her 'death,' the failed suicide attempt of 1953."

26   SEXTON, ANNE. "The Barfly Ought to Sing." In *Ariel Ascending:
       Writings about Sylvia Plath*. Edited by Paul Alexander. New York:
       Harper and Row, pp. 178-84.
            Reprint of 1966.B18*; 1970.A2*. Reprinted: in part: 1988.73.

27   SPIVACK, KATHLEEN. "Lear in Boston: Robert Lowell as
       Teacher and Friend." *Ironwood* (Spring): 76-92 passim.
            Discusses several of the poets in Lowell's 1958 writing seminar
       in Boston. Portrays Plath as "prim and quiet" but competitive, often
       "scathing" in her critiques of other students' work.

28   VENDLER, HELEN. "An Intractable Metal." In *Ariel Ascending:
       Writings about Sylvia Plath*. Edited by Paul Alexander. New York:
       Harper and Row, pp. 1-12.
            Reprint of 1982.59.

29   WAGNER, LINDA W. "Plath on Napoleon." *Notes on Contem-
       porary Literature* 15 (March): 6.
            Connects Plath's use of Napoleon Bonaparte in "The Swarm"
       to her recent reading of Hubert Cole's *Josephine*, which she had
       reviewed for *The New Statesman* six months before writing the poem.

Plath may have identified with Josephine's situation, which was similar to Plath's own.

30 ____."Sylvia Plath's Specialness in Her Short Stories." *Journal of Narrative Technique* 15 (Winter): 1-14.

Presents a close reading of several short stories to suggest that Plath was not "using factually autobiographical materials" but rather repeatedly examining the same "images and themes to give insight into her own view of herself, and into the problems and situations that troubled her most." Many female protagonists are "torn with the simple conflicts of having to excel within a culture that demands, from its women, submission rather than aggression and conformity rather than specialness." In that sense each protagonist is Plath herself.

1986

1 APPLEWHITE, JAMES. "Modernism and the Imagination of Ugliness." *Sewanee Review* 94 (Summer): 418-39 passim.

Uses Plath in a discussion about modernism as an example of the 1940's and 50's, an era "of the breakage of the artistic psyche." Comments on Plath's and others' tendency to long for a "psychic death and rebirth [which] becomes an overt personalized thrust toward suicide." Applies Freud's "Mourning and Melancholia" to Plath and her later poems. Concludes the section on Plath by stating that by the time of her death "modernism . . . had come to imply, for its most advanced poets, a self-subjection to a brutally imposed factuality."

2 BENNETT, PAULA. "Sylvia Plath: Fusion and the Divided Self." In *My Life a Loaded Gun*. Boston: Beacon Press, pp. 95-164.

Divides this chapter on Plath into three sections, entitled "The Mother Bond," "Bonds of Women," and "The Lioness." In the first, a biographical sketch of Plath's mother and a discussion of Plath's desperate attempts to please her are included. Aurelia Plath was determined to see, hear, and discuss only the positive aspects of life. Sylvia never felt capable of sharing her negative experiences with her mother and was forced to lead a dual life.

The second section expands upon this "duplicity of Plath's relationships to the world at large," especially during her high school and college years. *The Bell Jar* is used extensively to illuminate further this era of Plath's life. Concludes by commenting on Plath's obsession with finding the right man to make her life complete.

The last section focuses on the years between 1956, when she wed Ted Hughes, and 1963, the year of her death. The evolution of her poetic style and voice is discussed as emerging from the turmoil and conflict in her life as wife, mother, and poet. Several of the later poems are analyzed in detail.

3   CAWS, MARY ANN. "The Conception of Engendering: The Erotics of Editing." In *The Poetics of Gender*. Edited by Nancy K. Miller. New York: Columbia University Press, pp. 51-52.

Includes Ted Hughes as one example of an editor who, in a sense, actually engenders a writer's text, "making it presentable."

4   COLLECOTT, DIANA. "Mirror-Image: Images of Mirrors . . . In Poems by Sylvia Plath, Adrienne Rich, Denise Levertov and H.D." *Revue française d'études Americaines* 11 (November): 449-54.

Analyzes Plath's "Mirror" as a poem "that embod[ies] the female sense of being 'other in oneself' in images of mirroring."

5   FRIEL, JAMES P. "'The Bee Meeting' of Sylvia Plath." *Esprit* 2 (Spring): 142-45.

Asserts that "The Bee Meeting" concerns "the problem of the individual in society. In the poem, the individual remains subject to the 'mastery' of his/her society yet does not achieve a kind of triumph, which results from '*seeing* the charade or role-playing that pretends to be authentic or legitimate.'"

6   GUBAR, SUSAN. "'The Blank Page' and the Issues of Female Creativity." In *Gender Studies: New Directions in Feminist Criticism*. Edited by Judith Spector. Bowling Green, Ohio: Bowling Green State University Popular Press, pp. 10-29.

Mentions Plath on pp. 20-21. "At the end of *Ariel*, she is perfected into a statue. . . . The dialectic between perfection and blood distinction means finally that Plath's 'Words' are 'Axes' from whose rhythmic strokes she will never recover."

1986

7   JERABELK, MONIKA. "Sylvia Plath: Electra Inspired." In *Student Writers at Work: The Bedford Prizes*. Edited by Nancy Sommers and Donald McQuade. New York: St. Martin's Press, pp. 118-25.
     Analyzes the images of the father in Plath's work and connects aspects of Plath's life to the style and content of the poetry. The essay, which was written in 1984, won the Bedford Prize in Student Writing in 1985.

8   LINDBERG-SEYERSTED, BRITA. "Gender and Women's Literature: Thoughts on a Relationship Illustrated by the Cases of Emily Dickinson and Sylvia Plath." *American Studies in Scandinavia* 18:1-14.
     Discusses several ways in which being a woman shapes woman's art. "Femaleness is an important key to the work of [both Plath and Dickinson], but . . . it is not the only key."

9   MATOVICH, RICHARD M., ed. *A Concordance to the Collected Poems of Sylvia Plath*. New York: Garland Press, 623 pp.
     Lists alphabetically every word and the frequency of use in *The Collected Poems*. Also includes a listing of all the words in the concordance itself, in order of frequency.

10   PERLOFF, MARJORIE. "The Two Ariels: The (Re)Making of the Sylvia Plath Canon." In *Poems in Their Place*. Edited by Neil Fraistat. Chapel Hill: University of North Carolina Press, pp. 308-33.
     Points out that the *Ariel* Plath intended would have made a very different impression than did the one actually published by Ted Hughes. The intended volume, as Plath herself indicated, began with the word "love" and ended with the word "spring," thus concluding on "a note of hope." The volume published by Hughes, on the other hand, has supported critical assessments of Plath's suicide as "inevitable, . . . that it was brought on, not by her actual circumstances, but by her essential and seemingly incurable schizophrenia." Comments on the irony of a situation which places "the very man who is, in one guise or another," the subject of her poems in the position of their censor and publisher.

1986

11   PETERSON, RAI. "Sylvia Plath's Lunar Images: 'Metamorphoses of the Moon.'" *Journal of Mental Imagery* 10 (Summer): 103-12.

Presents a chronological explication of several poems in order to reveal the changes in Plath's use of moon imagery over time. In the earlier work, the moon is variously represented as "green cheese, supernatural light, and a symbol of death." In the poems written just before her death, the moon becomes Plath's soul.

12   SILVERMAN, M. A., and WILL, NORMAN P. "Sylvia Plath and the Failure of Emotional Self-Repair through Poetry." *Psychoanalytic Quarterly* 55: 99-129.

Examines the reasons that Plath's creative activity failed to heal her psyche and prevent her suicide. The "shared affective experience of poetry" should have connected her to others. Instead she remained alienated. When she turned "from traditional forms and mediated images [to] a more personal expressive art, she lost the shaping, controlling devices she had been using for self-containment and self-repair."

13   WAGNER, LINDA W. "Plath's *The Bell Jar* as Female *Bildungsroman*." *Women's Studies* 12 (February): 55-68.

Presents *The Bell Jar* as a "highly conventional *Bildungsroman*," as discussed by Jerome Buckley in his *Season of Youth*. "[I]ts principal elements are 'a growing up and gradual self-discovery,' 'alienation,' 'provinciality,' the larger society, 'the conflict of generations,' 'ordeal by love,' and 'the search for a vocation and a working philosophy.'" Each of these elements in Plath's novel is cited and described. Concludes by commenting on the generic differences "between female and male *bildungsroman*."

14   WALBURG, LORI. "Plath's Brasilia." *Explicator* 44 (Spring): 60-62.

Connects the images in "Brasilia" to icons and traditions in the Catholic Church and in Christianity in general. Suggests the possibility that the angels of the poem were drawn from the Crown of Thorns Cathedral in the city of Brasilia.

15   WOOD, DAVID. "Sylvia Plath and Anne Sexton." *Kyushu American Literature* 27:81-86.

Judges Plath's work as superior to Sexton's. Sexton "lacks the fertile creativity of Plath. Unlike Sexton, Plath eventually achieves the "necessary distance between writer and subject."

1987

1   BASSNETT, SUSAN. *Sylvia Plath*. Houndmills and London: Macmillan, 164 pp.

Begins with an overview of Plath's life and work. Each successive chapter presents a critical assessment of different aspects of Plath's work. The importance of family, of love, of "husband-worship," of "domestic crisis," and of "the struggle to survive" is discussed. Her struggle, in fact, has made Plath "another figure representative of a whole generation."

2   BLASING, MUTLU KONUK. "Sylvia Plath's Black Car of Lethe." In *American Poetry: The Rhetoric of Its Forms*. New Haven: Yale University Press, pp. 50-63.

Examines Plath's rhetorical strategies and maintains that her work follows from Poe. Examines Plath's "presentation of the self-destructive process of expression."

3   BRESLIN, PAUL. "Sylvia Plath: The Mythically Fated Self." In *The Psycho-Political Muse: American Poetry since the Fifties*. Chicago and London: University of Chicago Press, pp. 95-117.

Discusses Plath's work in terms of her "attempt to transform her life into myth." This goal, however, was problematic because she chose two almost mutually exclusive myths. In striving for the one, she focused on being the dutiful daughter, wife, and mother; for the other, the supreme artist/poet. What results is "a violent oscillation between extremes," as one myth negates the other. "The Moon and the Yew Tree" is analyzed as an example of one of Plath's "moments of balance in which the access to . . . personal pain has not tempted the poet to depend on the reader's . . . sympathy for that pain."

1987

4 DONOGHUE, DENIS. "Sylvia Plath." In *Reading America*. New York: Alfred A. Knopf, pp. 296-301.
Reprint of 1981.6.

5 FREEDMAN, WILLIAM. "Sylvia Plath's 'Mirror' of Mirrors." *Papers on Language and Literature* 23 (Winter): 56-69.
Offers "an alternative approach" to the various psychological interpretations of Plath's images of mirrors and of water as mirrors. "[T]he ultimate mirrors may be the utterances that contain them: mirrors that are not mere surfaces but depths, not mere reflectors but creative instruments whose principal mediation is on the protean act of mirroring itself."

6 MEYERS, JEFFERY. "Epilogue: Sylvia Plath." In *Manic Power: Robert Lowell and His Circle*. London: Macmillan, pp. 139-79.
Systematically describes the characteristics Plath shares with Roethke, Lowell, Berryman, and Jarrell. Maintains that Plath's poetry "derived its power from madness," and that she saw the poet as a sacrificial figure." Provides a brief biography of Plath.

7 MONTEFIORE, JAN. *Feminism and Poetry*. London and New York: Pandora, pp. 17-20.
Discusses the sexual significance of the flower imagery in Plath's "Poppies in July." The poem's speaker is "obsessed by jealousy. ... Conventional meanings are pushed to a savage, almost unrecognizable extreme." The analysis is one part of a broad discussion of feminist poets' use of flower images.

8 TABOR, STEPHEN. *Sylvia Plath: An Analytical Bibliography*. Westport, Conn.: Meckler, 268 pp.
Contains a list of all material written by and about Plath. Also includes physical descriptions of Plath's major and minor publications.

9 TIMMERMAN, JOHN H. "Plath's Mirror." *Explicator* 45 (Winter): 63-64.

1988

Cites C. G. Jung to explain Plath's poem. The "terrible fish" that rises to meet the aging woman who looks at her reflection in the lake represents "unconscious reality." Jung himself uses "mythic variations that associate the fish with feminine nature."

10   WAGNER, LINDA W. *Sylvia Plath: A Biography.* New York: Simon and Schuster, 282 pp.
        Utilizes hitherto unavailable journals and letters to tell the story of Plath's life. The significance of her death and her relationship with her mother are connected to the poet's long battle with emotional problems. The stress created by Plath's struggle to be both perfect scholar/poet and perfect wife/mother also contributed to her breakdown and eventual suicide.

1988

1   AIRD, EILEEN M. "'Poem for a Birthday' to *Three Women*: Development in the Poetry of Sylvia Plath." In *Sylvia Plath: The Critical Heritage*. Edited by Linda W. Wagner. London: Routledge and Kegan Paul, pp. 191-203.
        Reprint of 1979.2.

2   ___. "Review." In *Sylvia Plath: The Critical Heritage*. Edited by Linda W. Wagner. London: Routledge and Kegan Paul, pp. 136-39.
        Reprint of 1971.B2*.

3   "Along the Edge." In *Sylvia Plath: The Critical Heritage*. Edited by Linda W. Wagner. London: Routledge and Kegan Paul, pp. 58-60.
        Reprint of 1965.B8*.

4   ALVAREZ, A. "The Poet and the Poetess." In *Sylvia Plath: The Critical Heritage*. Edited by Linda W. Wagner. London: Routledge and Kegan Paul, pp. 34-35.
        Reprint of 1960.B1*.

5 ____. "Poetry in Extremis." In *Sylvia Plath: The Critical Heritage*. Edited by Linda W. Wagner. London: Routledge and Kegan Paul, pp. 55-57
Reprint of 1965.B1*.

6 ANNAS, PAMELA J. *A Disturbance in Mirrors: The Poetry of Sylvia Plath*. Westport, Conn.: Greenwood Press, 192 pp.
Traces the ways in which Plath's poetry grows out of the conflicts and paradoxes the poet experienced within herself. Much of her work is an exercise in redefinition of the self. Chronicles the struggles of the reborn self trying to survive in a depersonalized society.

7 AXELROD, STEVEN GOULD. "The Second Destruction of Sylvia Plath." In *Sylvia Plath: The Critical Heritage*. Edited by Linda W. Wagner. London: Routledge and Kegan Paul, pp. 313-19.
Reprint of 1985.5.

8 BERE, CAROL. *"Letters Home: Correspondence, 1950-1963."* In *Sylvia Plath: The Critical Heritage*. Edited by Linda W. Wagner. London: Routledge and Kegan Paul, pp. 219-22.
Reprint of 1977.3; 1984.4.

9 BERGONZI, BERNARD. "The Ransom Note." In *Sylvia Plath: The Critical Heritage*. Edited by Linda W. Wagner. London: Routledge and Kegan Paul, pp. 32-33.
Reprint of 1960.B2*.

10 BOYERS, ROBERT. "On Sylvia Plath." In *Sylvia Plath: The Critical Heritage*. Edited by Linda W. Wagner. London: Routledge and Kegan Paul, pp. 144-52.
Reprint of 1973.3.

11 BRANS, JO. "The Girl Who Wanted to Be God." In *Sylvia Plath: The Critical Heritage*. Edited by Linda W. Wagner. London:

Routledge and Kegan Paul, pp. 213-16.
Reprint of 1976.8; 1984.4.

12   BRINNING, JOHN MALCOLM. "Plath, Jarrell, Kinnell, Smith." In
      Sylvia Plath: The Critical Heritage. Edited by Linda W. Wagner.
      London: Routledge and Kegan Paul, pp. 8-9.
      Reprint of 1967.B2*.

13   "Chained to the Parish Pump." In *Sylvia Plath: The Critical Heritage*.
      Edited by Linda W. Wagner. London: Routledge and Kegan Paul, p.
      9.
           Reprint of 1967.B8*.

14   COTTER, JAMES FINN. "Women Poets: Malign Neglect?" In
      Sylvia Plath: The Critical Heritage. Edited by Linda W. Wagner.
      London: Routledge and Kegan Paul, pp. 182-83.
           Reprint of 1973.B5*.

15   COX, C.B. "Editorial." In *Sylvia Plath: The Critical Heritage*. Edited
      by Linda W. Wagner. London: Routledge and Kegan Paul, pp. 99-
      100.
           Reprint of A1966.3. See Appendix.

16   DALE, PETER. "O Honey Bees Come Build." In *Sylvia Plath: The
      Critical Heritage*. Edited by Linda W. Wagner. London: Routledge
      and Kegan Paul, pp. 62-68.
           Reprint of A1966.4. See Appendix.

17   DAVISON, PETER. "Inhabited by a Cry: The Lost Poetry of Sylvia
      Plath." In *Sylvia Plath: The Critical Heritage* Edited by Linda W.
      Wagner. London: Routledge and Kegan Paul, pp. 80-84.
           Reprint of 1966.B5*; 1984.9.

1988

18 DEJONG, MARY G. "Sylvia Plath and Sheila Ballantyne's *Imaginary Crimes*." *Studies in American Fiction* 16 (Spring): 27-38.
Discusses Ballantyne's *Imaginary Crimes* and Plath's "Daddy" as similar works in that both are examples of a daughter's struggle to free herself from her father in order to establish an independent identity. Suggests that "Daddy" was a source for *Imaginary Crimes*." Establishes several specific correspondences between the two works.

19 De LAURETIS, TERESA. "Rebirth in *The Bell Jar*." In *Sylvia Plath: The Critical Heritage* Edited by Linda W. Wagner. London: Routledge and Kegan Paul, pp. 124-34.
Reprint of 1976.18.

20 DUFFY, MARTHA. "Two Lives." In *Sylvia Plath: The Critical Heritage*. Edited by Linda W. Wagner. London: Routledge and Kegan Paul, pp. 216-19.
Reprint of 1975.7.

21 DUNN, DOUGLAS. "Damaged Instruments." In *Sylvia Plath: The Critical Heritage*. Edited by Linda W. Wagner. London: Routledge and Kegan Paul, pp. 139-42.
Reprint of 1971.B19*. Reprinted: 1984.12.

22 DYSON, A. E. "Reviews and Comments." Review of *The Colossus*. In *Sylvia Plath: The Critical Heritage*. Edited by Linda W. Wagner. London: Routledge and Kegan Paul, pp. 36-41.
Reprint of 1961.B2*; 1984.13.

23 EAGLETON, TERRY. "New Poetry." In *Sylvia Plath: The Critical Heritage*. Edited by Linda W. Wagner. London: Routledge and Kegan Paul, pp. 152-55.
Reprint of A1971.12. See Appendix.

24   FELDMAN, IRVING. "The Religion of One." In *Sylvia Plath: The Critical Heritage*. Edited by Linda W. Wagner. London: Routledge and Kegan Paul, pp. 84-88.
    Reprint of A1966.5. See Appendix.

25   FRASER, G. S. "Pass to the Centre." In *Sylvia Plath: The Critical Heritage*. Edited by Linda W. Wagner. London: Routledge and Kegan Paul, pp. 243-45.
    Reprint of 1977.17.

26   FULLER, ROY. "Book Reviews." In *Sylvia Plath: The Critical Heritage*. Edited by Linda W. Wagner. London: Routledge and Kegan Paul, pp. 35-36.
    Reprint of 1961.B3*.

27   FURBANK, P. N. "New Poetry." In *Sylvia Plath: The Critical Heritage*. Edited by Linda W. Wagner. London: Routledge and Kegan Paul, pp. 73-74.
    Reprint of 1965.B2*.

28   GILBERT, SANDRA M., and GUBAR, SUSAN. *No Man's Land*. New Haven: Yale University Press, pp. 61-62, 119-24.
    Discusses the ways Plath describes the "sexual battle that was not just intensely physical but also notably linguistic, with combat carried on through words, whispers, promises, vows." Briefly mentions Plath in several other parts of the book as well.

29   GRANT, DAMIAN. "*Winter Trees*." In *Sylvia Plath: The Critical Heritage*. Edited by Linda W. Wagner. London: Routledge and Kegan Paul, pp. 177-79.
    Reprint of 1972.B9*; 1984.15.

30 HAMILTON, IAN. "Poetry." In *Sylvia Plath: The Critical Heritage*. Edited by Linda W. Wagner. London: Routledge and Kegan Paul, pp. 48-51.
    Reprint of 1963.B4*.

31 HARRIS, MASON. "*The Bell Jar.*" In *Sylvia Plath: The Critical Heritage*. Edited by Linda W. Wagner. London: Routledge and Kegan Paul, pp. 107-13.
    Reprint of 1973.12; 1984.17.

32 HILL, DOUGLAS. "Living and Dying." In *Sylvia Plath: The Critical Heritage*. Edited by Linda W. Wagner. London: Routledge and Kegan Paul, pp. 234-37.
    Reprint of 1978.8; 1984.18.

33 HOMBERGER, ERIC. "The Uncollected Plath." In *Sylvia Plath: The Critical Heritage*. Edited by Linda W. Wagner. London: Routledge and Kegan Paul, pp. 187-91.
    Reprint of A1972.11. See Appendix.

34 HOWARD, RICHARD. Review of *The Colossus*. In *Sylvia Plath: The Critical Heritage*. Edited by Linda W. Wagner. London: Routledge and Kegan Paul, pp. 45-46.
    Reprint of 1963.B5*.

35 HOWES, VICTOR. "I Am Silver and Exact." In *Sylvia Plath: The Critical Heritage*. Edited by Linda W. Wagner. London: Routledge and Kegan Paul, pp. 142-43.
    Reprint of 1971.B23*.

36 HULSE, MICHAEL. "Formal Bleeding." In *Sylvia Plath: The Critical Heritage*. Edited by Linda W. Wagner. London: Routledge and Kegan Paul, pp. 291-93.
    Reprint of 1981.8.

37 JACKSON, MARNI. "In Search of the Shape Within." In *Sylvia Plath: The Critical Heritage*. Edited by Linda W. Wagner. London: Routledge and Kegan Paul, pp. 304, 306.
Reprint of 1982.21.

38 JEROME, JUDSON. "A Poetry Chronicle-Part I." In *Sylvia Plath: The Critical Heritage*. Edited by Linda W. Wagner. London: Routledge and Kegan Paul, pp. 44-45.
Reprint of 1963.B7*.

39 JONG, ERICA. "Letters Focus Exquisite Rage of Sylvia Plath." In *Sylvia Plath: The Critical Heritage*. Edited by Linda W. Wagner. London: Routledge and Kegan Paul, p. 9.
Reprint of 1975.15.

40 KAMEL, ROSE. "'Reach Hag Hands and Haul Me In'": Matrophobia in the Letters of Sylvia Plath." In *Sylvia Plath: The Critical Heritage*. Edited by Linda W. Wagner. London: Routledge and Kegan Paul, pp. 223-33.
Reprint of 1981.10.

41 KENNER, HUGH. "Arts and the Age, On *Ariel*." In *Sylvia Plath: The Critical Heritage*. Edited by Linda W. Wagner. London: Routledge and Kegan Paul, pp. 74-78.
Reprint of 1966.B9*.

42 KING, NICHOLAS. "Poetry: A Late Summer Roundup." In *Sylvia Plath: The Critical Heritage*. Edited by Linda W. Wagner. London: Routledge and Kegan Paul, p. 48.
Reprint of 1962.B4*.

43 KIRKHAM, MICHAEL. "Sylvia Plath." In *Sylvia Plath: The Critical Heritage*. Edited by Linda W. Wagner. London: Routledge and Kegan Paul, pp. 276-91.
Reprint of 1984.20.

1988

44   KLEIN, ELINOR. "A Friend Recalls Sylvia Plath." In *Sylvia Plath: The Critical Heritage.* Edited by Linda W. Wagner. London: Routledge and Kegan Paul, p. 27.
         Partial reprint of 1966.B10*.

45   KLEINSCHMIDT, EDWARD. "Shed, Unfinished Lives: Plath and Keats." *Centennial Review* 32 (Summer): 279-85.
         Compares and contrasts Plath and Keats, using both poets' letters. Focuses primarily on their life situations and early deaths.

46   KOPP, JANE BALTZELL. Excerpt of "'Gone, Very Gone Youth.'" In *Sylvia Plath: The Critical Heritage.* Edited by Linda W. Wagner. London: Routledge and Kegan Paul, p. 28.
         Partial reprint of 1977.28.

47   KRAMER, VICTOR A. "Life and Death Dialectics." In *Sylvia Plath: The Critical Heritage.* Edited by Linda W. Wagner. London: Routledge and Kegan Paul, pp. 161-64.
         Reprint of 1972.B15*.

48   KURTZMAN, MARY. "Plath's 'Ariel' and Tarot." *Centennial Review* 32 (Summer): 286-95.
         Establishes correspondences between the symbols, characters and personae in Plath's work and the figures in Tarot cards. Tarot's "ancient archetypal map becomes a natural inspiration to a poet."

49   LERNER, LAURENCE. "New Novels." Review of *The Bell Jar.* In *Sylvia Plath: The Critical Heritage.* Edited by Linda W. Wagner. London: Routledge and Kegan Paul, pp. 53-54.
         Reprint of 1963.B8*.

50   ____. "Sylvia Plath." In *Sylvia Plath: The Critical Heritage.* Edited by Linda W. Wagner. London: Routledge and Kegan Paul, pp. 259-62.
         Reprint of 1982.24; 1984.21.

51 LEVENSON, CHRISTOPHER. From a letter to Linda W. Wagner, 27 October 1984. In *Sylvia Plath: The Critical Heritage*. Edited by Linda W. Wagner. London: Routledge and Kegan Paul, pp. 29-30.
      Describes Plath as intense and sophisticated. She always seemed aware of "a sense of power, and of a larger, less controllable world."

52 LEVINE, MIRIAM. "*The Journals of Sylvia Plath*." In *Sylvia Plath: The Critical Heritage*. Edited by Linda W. Wagner. London: Routledge and Kegan Paul, pp. 308-12.
      Reprint of 1983.13.

53 LINENTHAL, MARK. "Sensibility and Reflection from the Poet's Corner." In *Sylvia Plath: The Critical Heritage*. Edited by Linda W. Wagner. London: Routledge and Kegan Paul, p. 47.
      Reprint of A1963.6. See Appendix.

54 MALOFF, SAUL. "Waiting for the Voice to Crack." In *Sylvia Plath: The Critical Heritage*. Edited by Linda W. Wagner. London: Routledge and Kegan Paul, pp. 103-7.
      Reprint of 1971.B36*.

55 MAYNARD, JOYCE. "Desperate Ladies." *Mademoiselle* 94 (January): 50, 52, 54.
      Reviews *Sylvia Plath: A Biography* by Linda Wagner-Martin, (See 1987.9), but also comments upon Plath's life. "It's too easy . . . to see [Ted] Hughes as the villain. . . . [Plath], too, . . . must have been an enormously difficult person to live with and be married to. . . . The greater error was Plath's, for imagining that any man would be enough to make her happy, to make her life."

56 MELANDER, INGRID. "Review." In *Sylvia Plath: The Critical Heritage*. Edited by Linda W. Wagner. London: Routledge and Kegan Paul, pp. 184-87.
      Reprint of A1971.33. See Appendix.

1988

57   MORRIS, IRENE. "Sylvia Plath at Newnham: A Tutorial Recollection." In *Sylvia Plath: The Critical Heritage*. Edited by Linda W. Wagner. London: Routledge and Kegan Paul, pp. 28-29.
        Partial reprint of 1975.20.

58   MYERS, E. LUCAS. "The Tranquilized Fifties." In *Sylvia Plath: The Critical Heritage*. Edited by Linda W. Wagner. London: Routledge and Kegan Paul, pp. 42-44.
        Reprint of 1962.B5*; 1984.26.

59   OATES, JOYCE CAROL. "*Winter Trees*." In *Sylvia Plath: The Critical Heritage*. Edited by Linda W. Wagner. London: Routledge and Kegan Paul, pp. 175-76.
        Reprint of 1972.B23*.

60   O'HARA, J. D. "An American Dream Girl." In *Sylvia Plath: The Critical Heritage*. Edited by Linda W. Wagner. London: Routledge and Kegan Paul, pp. 101-2.
        Reprint of 1971.B45*.

61   PATERNO, DOMENICA. "Poetry." In *Sylvia Plath: The Critical Heritage*. Edited by Linda W. Wagner. London: Routledge and Kegan Paul, pp. 135-36.
        Reprint of 1971.B46*.

62   PERLOFF, MARJORIE. "Sylvia Plath's *Collected Poems*." In *Sylvia Plath: The Critical Heritage*. Edited by Linda W. Wagner. London: Routledge and Kegan Paul, pp. 293-303.
        Reprint of 1981.17.

63   "Poems for the Good Hearted." In *Sylvia Plath: The Critical Heritage*. Edited by Linda W. Wagner. London: Routledge and Kegan Paul, p. 62.
        Reprint of 1965.B7*.

1988

64   PORTER, PETER. "Collecting Her Strength." In *Sylvia Plath: The Critical Heritage*. Edited by Linda W. Wagner. London: Routledge and Kegan Paul, pp. 155-57.
     Reprint of 1971.B48*; 1984.31.

65   PRATT, LINDA RAY. "'The Spirit of Blackness Is in Us....'" In *Sylvia Plath: The Critical Heritage*. Edited by Linda W. Wagner. London: Routledge and Kegan Paul, pp. 168-71.
     Reprint of 1973.B15*.

66   PRITCHARD, WILLIAM H. "An Interesting Minor Poet?" In *Sylvia Plath: The Critical Heritage*. Edited by Linda W. Wagner. London: Routledge and Kegan Paul, pp. 262-68.
     Reprint of 1981.18. Reprinted: 1984.32.

67   ROSENTHAL, M. L. "Metamorphosis of a Book." In *Sylvia Plath: The Critical Heritage*. Edited by Linda W. Wagner. London: Routledge and Kegan Paul, pp. 92-95.
     Reprint of 1967.B10*; 1984.33.

68   ____. "Poets of the Dangerous Way." In *Sylvia Plath: The Critical Heritage*. Edited by Linda W. Wagner. London: Routledge and Kegan Paul, pp. 60-62.
     Reprint of 1965.B12*.

69   "Russian Roulette." In *Sylvia Plath: The Critical Heritage*. Edited by Linda W. Wagner. London: Routledge and Kegan Paul, pp. 88-90.
     Reprint of 1966.B20*.

70   SAGE, LORNA. "Death and Marriage." In *Sylvia Plath: The Critical Heritage*. Edited by Linda W. Wagner. London: Routledge and Kegan Paul, pp. 237-43.
     Reprint of 1977.47.

1988

71 SCIGAJ, LEONARD M. "The Painterly Plath that Nobody Knows." *Centennial Review* 32 (Summer): 220-49.

Concentrates on Plath's early poetry, which has been dismissed and neglected by critics. The tremendous status enjoyed by the *Ariel* poems has unfairly "denigrate[d] the early poetry as apprentice work." In fact, however, Plath's early work "reveals an accomplished artist." Contrasts "[Judith] Kroll's assessment [in her *Chapters in a Mythology*] of Plath's de Chirico poems with the other seven poems Plath wrote in response to paintings [from] 1956 through 1959."

72 SCRUTON, ROGER. "Sylvia Plath and the Savage God." In *Sylvia Plath: The Critical Heritage.* Edited by Linda W. Wagner. London: Routledge and Kegan Paul, pp. 171-75.

Reprint of A1971.49. See Appendix.

73 SEXTON, ANNE. From "The Barfly Ought to Sing." In *Sylvia Plath: The Critical Heritage.* Edited by Linda W. Wagner. London: Routledge and Kegan Paul, pp. 30-31.

Partial reprint of 1966.B18*; 1970.A2*; 1985.26.

74 SHOOK, MARGARET L. "Sylvia Plath: The Poet and the College." In *Sylvia Plath: The Critical Heritage.* Edited by Linda W. Wagner. London: Routledge and Kegan Paul, pp. 114-24.

Reprint of A1972.29. See Appendix.

75 SKELTON, ROBIN. "Britannia's Muse Revisited." Review of *Ariel*. In *Sylvia Plath: The Critical Heritage.* Edited by Linda W. Wagner. London: Routledge and Kegan Paul, pp. 90-91.

Reprint of 1965.B14*.

76 SMITH, DAVE. "Sylvia Plath, The Electric Horse." In *Sylvia Plath: The Critical Heritage.* Edited by Linda W. Wagner. London: Routledge and Kegan Paul, pp. 268-76.

Reprint of 1982.53.

1988

77 SMITH, RAYMOND. "Late Harvest." In *Sylvia Plath: The Critical Heritage*. Edited by Linda W. Wagner. London: Routledge and Kegan Paul, pp. 179-81.
      Reprint of 1972.B34*.

78 SPENDER, STEPHEN. "Warnings from the Grave." In *Sylvia Plath: The Critical Heritage*. Edited by Linda W. Wagner. London: Routledge and Kegan Paul, pp. 69-73.
      Reprint of A1966.13. See Appendix; 1970.A2*.

79 TILLINGHAST, RICHARD. "Worlds of Their Own." In *Sylvia Plath: The Critical Heritage*. Edited by Linda W. Wagner. London: Routledge and Kegan Paul, pp. 79-80.
      Reprint of 1969.B9*.

80 TULIP, JAMES. "Three Women Poets." In *Sylvia Plath: The Critical Heritage*. Edited by Linda W. Wagner. London: Routledge and Kegan Paul, pp. 95-98.
      Reprint of A1967.6. See Appendix.

81 TYLER, ANNE. "'The Voice Hangs On, Gay, Tremulous.'" In *Sylvia Plath: The Critical Heritage*. Edited by Linda W. Wagner. London: Routledge and Kegan Paul, pp. 210-12.
      Reprint of 1976.65.

82 "Under the Skin." In *Sylvia Plath: The Critical Heritage*. Edited by Linda W. Wagner. London: Routledge and Kegan Paul, Paul, p. 52.
      Reprint of 1963.B9*.

83 Unsigned Review of *The Colossus*. In *Sylvia Plath: The Critical Heritage*. Edited by Linda W. Wagner. London: Routledge and Kegan Paul, p. 41.
      Reprint of 1961.B4*.

1988

84   VAN DYNE, SUSAN. "Rekindling the Past in Sylvia Plath's 'Burning the Letters.'" *Centennial Review* 32 (Summer): 250-65.
           Discusses the significance of the evolution of "Burning the Letters" through successive drafts. Plath's use of the reverse side of Ted Hughes's manuscripts and her appropriation of many of his images which she then "made to serve [her] own purposes, were her conscious effort to repair the rupture in her personal life." More than most of Plath's other poems "Burning the Letters" shows the importance of "biographical events and earlier texts" to the *Ariel* poems. "This poem . . . arraigns Hughes' old papers as the subject, and then, as if to overcome the threatening dominance of his words, Plath incorporates scraps of his poems into the new fabric of her story."

85   WAGNER, LINDA W. Introduction to *Sylvia Plath: The Critical Heritage*. Edited by Linda W. Wagner. London: Routledge and Kegan Paul, pp. 1-24.
           Gives an overview of the criticism on each of Plath's published volumes of poetry and fiction. Each work is dealt with separately. Also discusses "the battle over what confessional poetry is or was, and how influential it is or was to more contemporary poetry. . . ." Ends by asserting that because Ted Hughes destroyed or suppressed some of Plath's work, and because some of her material has been sealed in the Smith College Plath Collection until the year 2013, "a full and just assessment of her work is not possible at the present time."

86   ___. "The Journals of Sylvia Plath." In *Sylvia Plath: The Critical Heritage*. Edited by Linda W. Wagner. London: Routledge and Kegan Paul, pp. 306-8.
           Reprint of 1983.25.

87   ___, ed. *Sylvia Plath: The Critical Heritage*. London: Routledge and Kegan Paul, 332 pp.
           Contents: Elinor Klein's "A Friend Recalls Sylvia Plath"; Jane Baltzell Kopp's "'Gone, Very Gone Youth'"; Irene V. Morris's "Sylvia Plath at Newnham: A Tutorial Recollection"; Christopher Levenson's "From a Letter to Linda W. Wagner"; Anne Sexton's "The Barfly Ought to Sing"; Bernard Bergonzi, "The Ransom Note"; John Wain's "Farewell to the World"; A. Alvarez's "The Poet and the

Poetess"; Roy Fuller's "Review"; A. E. Dyson's "Review"; Unsigned Review; E. Lucas Myers's "The Tranquilized Fifities"; Judson Jerome's "A Poetry Chronicle–Part I"; Richard Howard's "Review"; Mark Linenthal's "Sensibility and Reflection from the Poet's Corner"; Nicholas King's "Poetry: A Late Summer Roundup"; Ian M. Hamilton's "Poetry"; Unsigned Review, "Under the Skin"; Laurence Lerner's "New Novels"; A. Alvarez's "Poetry in Extremis"; Unsigned Review, "Along the Edge"; M. L. Rosenthal's "Poets of the Dangerous Way"; Unsigned Review, "Poems for the Good-Hearted"; Peter Dale's "'O Honey Bees Come Build'"; Stephen Spender's "Warnings from the Grave"; P. N. Furbank's "New Poetry"; Hugh Kenner's "Arts and the Age, On *Ariel*"; John Malcolm Brinnin's "Plath, Jarrell, Kinnell, Smith"; Richard Tillinghast's "Worlds of Their Own"; Peter Davison's "Inhabited by a Cry: The Last Poetry of Sylvia Plath"; Irving Feldman's "The Religion of One"; Unsigned Review, "Russian Roulette"; Robin Skelton's "Review"; Unsigned Review, "Chained to the Parish Pump"; M. L. Rosenthal's "Metamorphosis of a Book"; James Tulip's "Three Women Poets"; C. B. Cox's "Editorial"; Stephen Wall's "Review"; J. D. O'Hara's "An American Dream Girl"; Saul Maloff's "Waiting for the Voice to Crack"; Mason Harris's "*The Bell Jar*"; Margaret L. Shook's "Sylvia Plath: The Poet and the College"; Teresa De Lauretis's "Rebirth in *The Bell Jar*"; Domenica Paterno's "Poetry"; Eileen M. Aird's "Review"; Douglas Dunn's "Damaged Instruments"; Victor Howes's "I Am Silver and Exact"; Robert Boyers's "On Sylvia Plath"; Terry Eagleton's "New Poetry"; Peter Porter's "Collecting Her Strength"; Paul West's "*Crossing the Water*"; Victor Kramer's "Life-and-Death Dialectics"; Unsigned Review, "A World in Disintegration"; Linda Ray Pratt's "'The Spirit of Blackness is in Us . . .'"; Roger Scruton's "Sylvia Plath and the Savage God"; Joyce Carol Oates's "*Winter Trees*"; Damian Grant's "*Winter Trees*"; Raymond Smith's "Late Harvest"; James Finn Cotter's "Women Poets: Malign Neglect?"; Ingrid Melander's "Review"; Eric Homberger's "The Uncollected Plath"; Eileen M. Aird's "'Poem for a Birthday' to *Three Women*: Development in the Poetry of Sylvia Plath"; Erica Jong's "Letters Focus Exquisite Rage of Sylvia Plath"; Anne Tyler's "'The Voice Hangs On, Gay, Tremulous'"; Jo Brans's "'The Girl Who Wanted to be God'"; Martha Duffy's "Two Lives"; Carol Bere's "*Letters Home: Correspondence 1950-1963*"; Rose Kamel's "'Reach Hag Hands and Haul Me In': Matrophobia in the Letters of Sylvia Plath"; Douglas Hill's "Living and Dying"; Lorna Sage's "Death and Marriage"; G. S. Fraser's "Pass to the Centre"; Melody Zajdel's "Apprenticed in a Bible of Dreams: Sylvia Plath's Short Stories"; Laurence Lerner's "Sylvia Plath"; William H. Pritchard's "An Interesting Minor Poet?";

1988

Dave Smith's "Sylvia Plath, the Electric Horse"; Michael Kirkham's "Sylvia Plath"; Michael Hulse's "Formal Bleeding"; Marjorie Perloff's "Sylvia Plath's *Collected Poems*"; Marni Jackson's "In Search of the Shape Within"; Linda W. Wagner's "*The Journals of Sylvia Plath*"; Miriam Levine's "*The Journals of Sylvia Plath*"; Steven Gould Axelrod's "The Second Destruction of Sylvia Plath."

88 WAIN, JOHN. "Farewell to the World." In *Sylvia Plath: The Critical Heritage*. Edited by Linda W. Wagner. London: Routledge and Kegan Paul, p. 33.
    Reprint of 1961.B6*.

89 WALL, STEPHEN. Review of *The Bell Jar*. In *Sylvia Plath: The Critical Heritage*. Edited by Linda W. Wagner. London: Routledge and Kegan Paul, p. 100.
    Reprint of A1966.15. See Appendix.

90 WEST, PAUL. "*Crossing the Water*." In *Sylvia Plath: The Critical Heritage*. Edited by Linda W. Wagner. London: Routledge and Kegan Paul, pp. 157-61.
    Reprint with different title of A1972.33. See Appendix. Reprint of 1984.42.

91 WOLFF, GEOFFREY. "*The Bell Jar*." In *Sylvia Plath: The Critical Heritage*. Edited by Linda W. Wagner. London: Routledge and Kegan Paul, p. 113.
    Reprint of A1971.56. See Appendix.

92 "A World in Disintegration." In *Sylvia Plath: The Critical Heritage*. Edited by Linda W. Wagner. London: Routledge and Kegan Paul, pp. 165-67.
    Reprint of 1971.B34*.

1988

93   ZAJDEL, MELODY. "Apprenticed in a Bible of Dreams: Sylvia Plath's Short Stories." In *Sylvia Plath: The Critical Heritage*. Edited by Linda W. Wagner. London: Routledge and Kegan Paul, pp. 245-58.

   Reprint of 1984.45.

Appendix

1947

1   "Wellesley Club Awards and School Letters Given at Junior High School Final Assembly." *Townsman* (Wellesley, Mass.), 3 July, p. 4.
     Mentions Plath's ninth grade award for "excellence in written and oral expression." She was the only student in the school's history to earn "enough credits" for six awards. She was also recognized for maintaining straight A's and for punctuality.

1948

1   "Wellesley High School Students Win High Honors in National Atlantic School Contest." *Townsman* (Wellesley, Mass.), 3 June, p. 12.
     Notes Plath's award for two poems given by the judges of what "is considered the foremost literary contest for secondary schools in this country."

1953

1   "Beautiful Smith Girl Missing at Wellesley." *Boston Daily Globe*, 25 August, pp. 1, 9.
     Announces Plath's disappearance from home and details the search efforts underway. Points out that at Smith College Plath was well-known for her "brilliance, creative talent, and initiative," and that she was at the top of her class.

2   "Carry On Search for Plath Girl." *Daily Hampshire Gazette*, 26 August, pp. 1, 3.

       Reports on the continued search for Plath after her disappearance from home. Aurelia Plath explains that her daughter had been distressed over her recent inability "to produce creatively."

3   "Condition Good of Smith Senior Who Took Pills." *Daily Hampshire Gazette*, 27 August, p. 3.

       Reports on Plath's condition in the Wellesley-Newton Hospital after her suicide attempt and subsequent discovery in the basement of her mother's home.

4   "Day-Long Search Fails to Locate Plath Girl." *Boston Daily Globe*, 26 August, pp. 1, 11.

       Gives details of the continuing search for the missing Plath. Her mother expresses doubts that her daughter would contact any of her acquaintances because of her depressed mood.

5   "Hunt for Missing Smith Honor Student Who Left on Long Hike Fruitless." *Daily Hampshire Gazette*, 25 August, pp. 1, 16.

       Reports on the search for Plath after she disappeared from home. Smith College officials expressed fear that Plath might have re-fractured her ankle, previously broken in a skiing accident.

6   "Missing Smith Girl Worried." *Boston Post*, 26 August, pp. 1, 13.

       An account of Plath's disappearance from her mother's home in Wellesley. Her mother states that her daughter had "'lost confidence in herself.'"

7   NELSON, NEVA, and WAGNER, JANET. "Jobiographies." *Mademoiselle* 37 (August): 252-55, 377-79.

       Explains the role of guest editors at *Mademoiselle*. Includes Plath's publishing history.

8   "Police, Boy Scouts Hunt Missing Smith Student." *Boston Evening Globe*, 25 August, pp. 1, 9.

Reports on the search for Plath after her first suicide attempt. Mrs. Plath is quoted as saying that Sylvia was nearing nervous collapse because "she has set standards for herself that are almost unattainable." The family doctor has recommended that Sylvia "devote less time to academic activities."

9   "Sleeping Pills Missing with Wellesley Girl." *Boston Herald*, 26 August, p. 1.

Gives an account of the search for Plath after she disappeared from her mother's home.

10   "Smith Correspondent for Gazette Honored." *Daily Hampshire Gazette*, 29 May, pp. 1, 12.

Reports on Plath selection as a guest editor for *Mademoiselle*, and lists her literary accomplishments.

11   "Smith Girl Recovering from Pills." *Boston Post*, 27 August, pp. 1, 4.

An account of the discovery of Plath in a "wood-storage area" in the cellar of her home, a nearly empty bottle of sleeping pills at her side.

12   "Smith Student Found Alive in Cellar." *Boston Evening Globe*, 26 August, pp. 1, 6.

Reports on the disappearance and discovery of Plath after her first suicide attempt. Mrs. Plath attributes her daughter's depression to a "temporary inability to turn out creative writing."

13   "Sylvia Plath Found in Good Condition." *Townsman* (Wellesley, Mass.), 27 August, p. 1.

Reports the discovery of Plath in the basement of her home after having swallowed "what is considered a lethal dose of sleeping pills."

14   "Wellesley Girl Found in Cellar." *Boston Herald*, 27 August, pp. 1, 2.

Gives an account of Plath's first suicide attempt. Plath was found behind a stack of firewood in the basement of her family's home.

Also discovered was a bottle containing 8 of the 50 sleeping pills it originally contained.

1955

1   CHRISTIAEN, CHRIS. "Poet on College Time." *Mademoiselle* 41 (August): 49, 52, 62.
     Describes Mount Holyoke's annual inter-collegiate poetry contest, of which "Plath was one of two winners. When interviewed, she said that college was "wonderfully conducive" to writing poetry. She also expressed impatience for graduation when she could go to Cambridge on a Fulbright.

2   HANDY, MARY. "Judges Hear Glasscok Poetry Contestants." *Christian Science Monitor*, 18 April, p. 2.
     A report on Plath's reading of her own work in a poetry contest at Mount Holyoke College.

3   "Miss Plath Reads Poetry in College Competition." *Townsman* (Wellesley, Mass.), 21 April, p. 6.
     Gives an account of the poetry contest at Mount Holyoke College in which Plath read her work. The judges were Marianne Moore, Wallace Fowlie, and John Ciardi.

4   "Miss Plath's Degree Is Summa Cum Laude." *Townsman* (Wellesley, Mass.), 9 June, p. 11.
     Reports Plath's many achievements and awards upon her graduation from Smith College.

1957

1   "Ex-Gazette Writer Returns as Smith Faculty Member." *Daily Hampshire Gazette*, 16 September, p. 3.
     Reports on Plath's return to Smith College to teach English.

2   HOBSON, HAROLD. "A Good Home." *Sunday Times*, 17 March, p. 19.

Comments on Plath's poem "Spinster" as a lead-in to a review of a performance of *As You Like It*. Calls the poem a "sharp-edged, memorable, precise . . . statement of the refusal of love."

1959

1   ROBINS, CORINNE. "Four Young Poets." *Mademoiselle* 48 (January): 34-35, 85.

Profiles of Sylvia Plath and Ted Hughes during the time they spent in the U.S. teaching at Smith College and the University of Massachusetts, respectively. Quotes Plath on her marriage to Hughes and her opinion of teaching.

1960

1   "Short Shorts." *John O'London's* 3 (17 November): 644.

Review of *The Colossus*. These 50 poems should "arouse a great deal of interest" in England.

2   "Sylvia Plath Publishes Her Verse." *Townsman* (Wellesley, Mass.), 14 April, p. 13.

Notes the forthcoming publication of *The Colossus*. The remainder of the article is devoted to Plath's husband, Ted Hughes.

1961

1   CLARKE, AUSTIN. "Three Poets." *Irish Times*, 7 January, p. 6.

Review of *The Colossus*. Plath "catch[es] up imagery wherever she goes." Occasionally her "vigour and verbal impact" are a bit overwhelming for the "European climate."

2   "The Critic, the Translator, and Poems Ancient and Modern." *Times*, 23 February, p. 15.

Review of *The Colossus* and three books by other authors. Plath "turns attention decisively outward" in her poems.

1962

1   Review of *The Colossus. Booklist and Subscription Books Bulletin* 59 (1
     November): 200.
         The "vigor and rhythm" of these poems are similar to that of
     "Anglo-Saxon poetry." The mundane and the every day are portrayed
     with "originality and fresh insight."

2   W[HITTEMORE], R[EED]. Review of *The Colossus. Carleton
     Miscellany* 3 (Fall): 89.
         Praises the volume mostly for its evidence of a finely honed
     craft. Plath writes "in the best modern tradition of well-wrought verse."

1963

1   BENEDICT, L. Review of *The Bell Jar. Sunday Telegraph*, 27 January,
     p. 9.
         Gives a brief summary of the plot of the novel, which is called
     "disturbing and moving."

2   BURGESS, ANTHONY. "Transatlantic Englishmen." *Observer*, 27
     January, p. 22.
         Review of *The Bell Jar*. The theme of emotional breakdown is
     explored through a "mature fictional approach." Instead of succumbing
     to "sensationalism," the author maintains "sensitivity and decorum."

3   FANE, VERNON. Review of *The Bell Jar. Sphere*, 26 January, p. 143.
         Gives a brief plot synopsis. Esther Greenwood's depression did
     not have a cause, "except possibly boredom – that enemy of the
     intelligent young."

4   FAULCONBRIDGE, FAITH. "American Surprises." *Glasgow Herald*,
     17 January, p. 9.
         Review of *The Bell Jar*, an admirable first novel, "enjoyable"
     despite its depressing subject matter because of its "detached humour,
     sensitive awareness, and . . . sheer zest."

5   HARDY, H. FORSYTH. Review of *The Bell Jar*. *Scotsman*, 26
     January, 'Week-End Magazine,' p. 6.
          The novel is "a remarkable achievement" because its writing is
     "imaginative," precise, lucid, "sharp, . . . penetrating" and filled with
     pleasurable "poetic image[s]."

6   LINENTHAL, MARK. "Sensibility and Reflection from the Poet's
     Corner." *San Francisco Sunday Chronicle*, 10 March, "This World"
     section, p. 33.
          Reviews *The Colossus*, pronouncing the poems "feminine [but]
     never effeminate." Predicts Plath will become a "major American
     voice." Reprinted: 1988.53.

7   MILLAR, RUBY. "In the Good Old Days." *Derbyshire Times*, 15
     February, p. 17.
          Review of *The Bell Jar*. The author displays a "surety of aim
     and startling deftness of phrase," rare qualities for American writers.

8   "New Fiction." *London Times*, 24 January, p. 13.
          Review of *The Bell Jar* and four books by other authors. Offers
     a brief summary of the plot and judges the heroine's "condition [as not]
     painfully serious."

9   "'A Poet's Epitaph' Honors the Late Sylvia Plath Hughes." *Townsman*
     (Wellesley, Mass.), 7 March, p. 3.
          Gives an account of the article by A. Alvarez, which was
     published in the *London Observer* on February 17, 1963. See 1963. B1*.

10   SIMON, JOHN. "More Brass than Enduring." In *Acid Test*. New York:
     Stein and Day, pp. 236-52.
          Reprint of 1962.B7*.

11   "Sylvia Plath Hughes." *Townsman* (Wellesley, Mass.), 21 February, p. 4.
          An obituary notice. The cause of death is listed as "virus
     pneumonia."

1964

1   GUTTMAN, ALLEN. "Love and Death and Dachau: Recent Poets."
     Studies on the Left 4 (Spring): 98-109.
          Discusses Plath and seven other writers. The *Colossus* poems
     "are most powerful when most autobiographical. And, finally, it is
     through autobiography that some of them move from private to public."

2   KELL, RICHARD. "Correspondence." *Critical Quarterly* 6 (Autumn):
     276.
          A letter to the editor responding to "After the Tranquilized
     Fifties." Takes issue with the ideas set forth in that essay. (See
     1964.B1*.)

3   LUCIE-SMITH, EDWARD. "A Murderous Art?" *Critical Quarterly* 6
     (Winter): 355-63.
          Comments on A. Alvarez's use of the phrase "a murderous art"
     to describe some of Plath later poems. As an art, poetry has made the
     unfortunate move toward narcissism; the artist, and human beings in
     general, toward a "faith in the infinite potentialities of the human
     creature." This response is largely the result of the breakdown in
     religious faith. The argument is not focused on Plath, but on the
     movement toward confessional, or personal, poetry.

1965

1   JOHNSON, B. S. "Measure, Chaos, and Indifference." *Ambit* 24:45-46.
          Review of *Ariel*. Although the poems are "overwhelmingly
     moving," their value to readers is negligible because they are so
     intensely private and because "after all, they did not save her, did they?"

1966

1   ALVAREZ, A. "Sylvia Plath." *TriQuarterly* 7 (Fall): 65-74.
          Reprint of 1963.B2*. Reprinted: 1969.B1*; 1970.A2*.

2   BURKE, HERBERT C. Review of *Ariel*. *Library Journal* 91 (1 June): 2851.

    These powerful poems describe the times in which we live, when "violent power looms *contra* man's fragile being more relentlessly than ever violent power has." Despite the taut emotion, Plath maintains "near-total" poetic control.

3   COX, C. B. "Editorial." *Critical Quarterly* 8 (Autumn): 195.

    Review of *The Bell Jar*. Maintains that the novel is so tied in with the *Ariel* poems that separating them is impossible. Because the tone becomes progressively more personal, the later sections of the novel are less successful than the earlier ones. Reprinted: 1988.15.

4   DALE, PETER. "'O Honey Bees Come Build.'" *Agenda* 4 (Summer): 49-55.

    The *Ariel* poems are "condensed, elliptical, and autobiographical," and as such places any literary critic in a dilemma: Deprived of the details of the circumstances in which they were written, readers may find the poems "impenetrable," yet to intrude upon the poet's "privacies" would be discourteous. Occasionally Plath is compared to Keats. "The main conflict in the book lies with her ambitions . . . as a poet and the soul-destroying mundanity of life as a mother and wife." Plath frequently sees death "in romantic terms" as the "way out of her dilemma." Reprinted: 1988.16.

5   FELDMAN, IRVING. "The Religion of One." *Book Week*, 19 June, p. 3.

    Describes the *Ariel* poems as "brilliant, vivid, hysterical, insane, isolated, bursting with revulsion, pain, and hatred." Only six of them, the bee and bee-keeping poems, reveal the poet on "this side of [cultural and personal] madness." Reprinted: 1988.24.

6   FRIEDBERG, MARTHA. "With Feeling and Color." *Chicago Tribune*, 26 June, "Books Today" section, p. 6.

    Review of *Ariel*. The poems are the product of the struggle between Plath's enormous talent and her "madness." She displays two obsessions: her father's death and her own death. The verses gleam with intense color and sound.

7   KENNY, HEBERT A. "Sylvia Plath's *Ariel*: Triumph Over Tragedy."
      Boston Globe, 29 May, p. A-38.
              Review of *Ariel*. Compares Plath to Thomas Chatterton and
      John Keats. Her poetry is "confessional and confined," filled with death.
      Ariel is much more powerful than her earlier volume, *The Colossus*.

8   PITT, VALERIE. "Isolated Case." *Sunday Telegraph*, 25 September, p.
      11.
              Maintains that *The Bell Jar* cannot accurately be called a novel
      because it is not actually "about relationships." The story of Esther's
      descent into madness is told extremely objectively, almost to the point
      of disinterestedness. The book is evidence of Plath's great talent,
      making the reader regret, once again, the author's early death.

9   Review of *Ariel*. *Choice* 3 (October): 650.
              Captures the "sweet ague of man in the 1960s through
      poetically precise language that shocks and sears yet oddly instructs and
      imparts a desperate joy in living."

10   Review of *Ariel*. *Kirkus Reviews* 34 (15 March): 351.
              These poems contain "fragments of . . . biography" and are
      dominated by death. The poems specifically about death "have a
      splendor, a purity and violence that is far beyond merely personal
      statement."

11   ROSENTHAL, M. L. "Blood and Plunder." *Spectator* 217 (30
      September): 418.
              Reviews *The Bell Jar*, "an inexpert, uneven novel, but [with]
      magnificent sections whose candour and revealed suffering will haunt
      anyone's memory."

12   SEALY, DOUGLAS. Review of *Ariel*. *Dublin Magazine* 5 (Summer):
      92-93.
              Characterizes the poems as expressions of "life [as] but a
      metaphor for dying. . . ." The distance between the poet and her subject
      is never great enough.

13 SPENDER, STEPHEN. "Warnings from the Grave." *New Republic* 23
     (June): 25-26.
          Perceives the *Ariel* poems as "visionary." Briefly compares
     Plath's poems to the poems of St. John of the Cross. Their power is not
     merely "an identifiable poetic personality expressing herself," but is her
     ability to "turn our horrors and our achievements into the same witches'
     brew." Reprinted: 1970.A2*; 1988.78.

14 STEINER, GEORGE. "Dying Is an Art." *Smith Alumnae Quarterly* 57
     (Winter): 85-87.
          Reprint of 1965.B16*.

15 WALL, STEPHEN. Review of *The Bell Jar*. *Observer*, 11 September, p.
     27.
          Notes the "extraordinary" objectivity Plath maintains in spite of
     "the nature of the material." Reprinted: 1988.89.

1967

1   ALDRICH, ELIZABETH. "Sylvia Plath's 'The Eye-Mote': An
     Analysis." *Harvard Advocate* 101 (May): 4-7.
          Discusses "The Eye-Mote" as a prime example of the way in
     which the "forces of the fragmented mind are expressed as absolute in
     [Plath's] poetry: purity and corruption, innocence and guilt, eternity,
     and the forces of change." Experience is "disciplined" and manipulated
     expertly throughout the poem.

2   DAVIS, STUART A. "The Documentary Sublime: The Posthumous
     Poetry of Sylvia Plath." *Harvard Advocate* 101 (May): 8-12.
          Discusses the "posthumous" quality of Plath's poems. Ponders
     such questions as, "should we blame the fact of her death for intruding
     on a reading of her poems? Or should we welcome it as support from
     the secular arm? ... Is [the poems'] 'finality' ... really of an esthetic
     sort?"

3   Review of *Ariel*. *Booklist* 63 (15): 613.
          Displays the poet's "sensitivity to ordinary human rela-
     tionships."

4   Review of *The Bell Jar. Books and Bookmen* 12 (February): 57.

        The novel fails to measure up to Plath's poetry. However, the author does "combine fresh metaphor with a reasonable control of her subject."

5   STEPHENS, ALAN. Review of *Ariel. Denver Quarterly* 1 (Winter): 110-12.

        The volume is melodramatic and "sensational." Plath's craft is "wonderfully spare." She is a "formidable rhetorician."

6   TULIP, JAMES. "Three Women Poets." *Poetry Australia* 19 (December): 35-37.

        The reissue of *The Colossus* is confirmation that making "the personal self of the poet the subject of the poem" has become a major trend of the 1960s. Compares and contrasts Plath with Robert Lowell, "but the problem remains that Miss Plath's poetry can never make a full and vital connection with objects." Reprinted: 1988.80.

1968

1   BRINK, ANDREW. "Sylvia Plath and the Art of Redemption." *Alphabet* 25 (December): 48-69.

        Maintains that the "redemptive symbolism" in the *Ariel* poems, though "imagistically potent," are ineffective. Regeneration, renewal, and affirmation are never achieved. Plath, like many other artists, "embark[ed] on a self-destructive journey which might have brought rebirth," but did not. The desire for rebirth is present in the poetry, but there is "no source of outside energy to activate the archetypes [of regeneration] – no love and no forgiveness." Thus, Plath's poems "resound in their own isolation."

2   EDEL, LEON. Letter to the Editor. *Times Literary Supplement*, 7 November, p. 1251.

        Maintains that literary critics should not attempt to diagnose writers psychoanalytically. The letter responds specifically to a previous one by David Holbrook in which he discusses Olwyn Hughes's objection to his proposed book, *Dylan Thomas and Sylvia Plath and the Symbolism of Schizoid Suicide*.

3   FEDERMAN, RAYMOND. "Poèmes par Sylvia Plath." *Esprit* 36 (May): 823-27.
     Review of *Ariel*. The two primary images in Plath's poetry are death, toward which she moved inexorably everyday, and the image of the father who died too soon. It is impossible to separate Plath's work from her psychology and obsession. In French.

4   HOLBROOK, DAVID. Letter to the Editor. *Times Literary Supplement*, 7 November, p. 1251.
     Responds to a previous (31 October) letter by Olwyn Hughes concerning her objections to Holbrook's book (A1968.5). Holbrook justifies his theory that "at the heart of Sylvia Plath's anguish there is . . . false logic held by a 'self,' which was no doubt a part of the whole woman, but somehow turned against herself, with dreadful consequences." Some of the poetry comes from one "self" and some from the other. Accuses Olwyn Hughes of trying to "suppress" this theory.

5   HUGHES, OLWYN. Letter to the Editor. *Times Literary Supplement*, 14 November, p. 1281.
     Responds to a 7 November letter by David Holbrook (A1968.4). Miss Hughes refutes Holbrook's contention that she is trying to "'suppress'" his book. She maintains she has never implied that Holbrook was "a poor literary critic," only that where Sylvia Plath is concerned, "he is either misinformed or deliberately misleading."

6   ____. "Sylvia Plath." *Times Literary Supplement*, 31 October, p. 1225.
     Responds to a previous letter written by David Holbrook (A1968.4). Denies Holbrook's assertion that she refused to give him permission to discuss Plath. Admits she did refuse him permission to quote from copyrighted material because she felt that Holbrook was misrepresenting both Plath and her work in his book.

7   Review of *Ariel*. *Publishers Weekly* 194 (26 August): 273.
     The collection is "extraordinary and brief." Mentions that it "was one of the American Library Association's Notable Books of 1966."

1969

1   D[AVIS], D[OUGLAS] M. "More on the Poetry Shelves." *National Observer* 8 (17 March): 21.
      A review of *The Colossus and Other Poems*, "an inexpensive reprint of her first book." The work is good, "but no match for *Ariel*."

2   HEDBERG, JOHANNES. "Sylvia Plath." In *Poets of Our Time: English Poetry from Yeats to Sylvia Plath*. Stockholm: Almqvist and Wiksell, pp. 164-71.
      Provides a gloss and close linguistic analysis of Plath's "Morning Song" and "Wuthering Heights." The poems themselves appear on pp. 162-63.

3   HOLBROOK, DAVID. "Sylvia Plath and the Problem of Violence in Art." *Cambridge Review* 90 (7 February): 249-50.
      Discusses Plath's "schizoid tendencies" in an explication of her poem "Tulips." She eventually became unable "to distinguish between . . . life and death."

4   HOMBERGER, ERIC. "I Am I." *Cambridge Review* 90 (7 February): 251-52.
      Discusses Plath's early work as examples of her experience as a "rather pained victim of a dislocation in the world around her."

5   RABAN, JONATHAN. "Exactitudes." *New Statesman* 78 (28 November): 783-84.
      Review of *Penguin Modern Stories 2*, in which Plath's "The Fifteen Dollar Eagle" appears. Summarizes the plot and calls the story a "gem." "Social and linguistic enclosure are brilliantly blended to make a rhetoric that works with the containment and singly directed force of a poem."

1970

1   ALVEREZ, A. "Sylvia Plath: The Cambridge Collection." In *The Cambridge Mind*. Edited by Eric Homberger, William Janeway, and Simon Schama. London: Jonathon Cape, pp. 299-303.
      Reprint of 1969.B2*.

2   POULIN, A., Jr. "Contemporary American Poetry: The Radical Tradition." *Concerning Poetry* 3 (Fall): 5-21.
      Discusses the differences and similarities between modernist and contemporary poetry, using several representative poets. Contemporary poetry is "more intimate and personal," necessitating some knowledge of the poet's biography. "Personal-confessional poets" like Plath "reveal . . . the deteriorating self speaking in a chosen voice." She uses irony, however, "to temper the intensity of emotion and suffering." She has replaced "ancient mythology [with] more recent history for [a] mythic background."

1971

1   B., R. "The Earlier Plath." *Plain Dealer*, 24 October, p. F-12.
      Review of *Crossing the Water*. Although these "'transitional poems'" include themes of love and the joy of motherhood, the "larger subject is . . . obsession with death." Plath is so deft at conveying emotion that the poems are "grim reading."

2   BAUERLE, RUTH. "Plath, at Last." *Plain Dealer*, 25 April, p. H-7.
      Review of *The Bell Jar*. The reader is constantly "aware of the distance between [Esther] and all other characters." What is needed is a careful biography of Plath to enable us to separate in *The Bell Jar* "what is beautiful autobiography and what has been transmuted by art into the structure of fiction."

3   "Book World Picks Fifty Notable Books of 1971." *Washington Post*, 5 December, p. 5.
      Review of *The Bell Jar*, a "harrowing" novel in which the heroine "is a female Doppelgänger of Holden Caulfield."

4   BOULANGER, GHISLAINE. Review of *The Bell Jar*. *Book-of-the-Month Club News*. (May): 5.
       Gives a summary of the plot and adds that the novel "affords insight into Sylvia Plath's death ... and adds a new dimension to the anguished voice that speaks through her poetry."

5   BRUSS, ELIZABETH WISSMAN. "Sylvia Plath: *Crossing the Water*." *Michigan Daily*, 13 November, p. 5.
       A Review of *Crossing the Water*. These poems are "inferior" to those of *Ariel*, but they have the advantage of being far enough removed from her suicide to be viewed as something more than the "relics" of death. The poems prove that Plath did not "foresee any future for her life [or] for her art."

6   BYRD, SCOTT. "Poet Draws Sad, Baleful Portrait of a Breakdown." *Charlotte Observer*, 18 April, p. F-8.
       Review of *The Bell Jar*. Marketing the book as a "high-class *Valley of the Dolls*" does it a disservice. Except for author's tendency toward "insubstantial characterization of the heroine," the book is "accomplished, witty, and very moving."

7   CLAIR, WILLIAM F. "A Summer of Her Discontent." *Washington Post*, 13 April, pp. C-1, 5.
       Review of *The Bell Jar*. The book is more a "psychological diary" than a polished work of fiction. Includes a brief summary of the plot.

8   "A Conversation with Robert Lowell." *Review* 26 (Summer): 10-29.
       Mentions Sylvia Plath as one of the only four women poets as good as "our best men." The others are Emily Dickinson, Marianne Moore, and Elizabeth Bishop. Plath learned from Anne Sexton.

9   De FEO, RONALD. Review of *The Bell Jar*. *Modern Occasions* 1 (Fall): 624-25.
       Describes *The Bell Jar* as "beautifully written" but "badly flawed," a book which is not as important as some other critics have suggested. Despite its autobiographical nature, the events are "unconvincing" and the novel as a whole "lacks density."

10   DICKEY, JAMES. "Spinning the Crystal Ball." In *Sorties: Journals and New Essays*. New York: Doubleday, pp. 190-91.

Criticizes confessional poetry, especially Plath's poetry, not because it exposes "the horrible depths everyone has" but because it does not go far enough in its exposure. Plath's work is too "slick," "glib," too "literary" in the negative sense of that word to offer a genuine portrayal of "real life."

11   DUDAR, HELEN. "From Book to Cult." *New York Post*, 2 September, pp. 3, 38.

Review of *The Bell Jar*. Reports that the "most fervent Plath fans" are sometimes obsessively involved in her life and death; however, *The Bell Jar*'s popularity rests upon something more substantial than mere "Plathism." Full of "wit [and] agony, the book represents recognizable experience." Many young women see themselves as Esther Greenwood.

12   EAGLETON, TERRY. "New Poetry." *Stand* 13; no. 1 (1971-72): 76.

Analyzes the images in *Crossing the Water*. The poems "have a rich and easy beauty beyond much that is achieved in [either *The Colossus* or *Ariel*]." Reprint of 1988.23.

13   FULLER, JOHN. "Waiting for Ariel." *Listener* 85 (3 June): 728-29.

Examines the poems in *Crossing the Water*. Measures them against those in both *The Colossus* and *Ariel* and shows how they serve as a bridge between the two.

14   GONZALES, LAURENCE. "Sylvia Plath, Crossing Over." *Chicago Daily News*, 9-10 October, 'Panorama' section, p. 12.

A review of *Crossing the Water*. The poems in this volume "are the dregs of Miss Plath's 'Colossus,' and what was left behind when she moved on to 'Ariel.'" The blame belongs not to the poet, but to the collector. That this is all of her remaining work is unlikely. Thus, better selections could have been made.

15   GOTTLIEB, ANNIE. Review of *The Bell Jar*. *Juris Doctor* 1 (April): 41.

In the years since it was first published in England, *The Bell Jar* has been "'politicized.'" Instead of focusing on madness, readers now focus on and identify with "the pressure that produced" the madness. Esther Greenwood has become "a brilliant prophet of the women's uprising."

16 GREEN, MARTIN. "Of Pigs and People." *Sunday Telegraph*, 6 June, p. 10.

A review of *Crossing the Water*. The volume is poignant, but one wonders "how Sylvia Plath would have developed as a poet had she lived on to write about more-than-immediate sensations."

17 HANLIN, WILLIAM C. "The Fragmentation that Precedes Suicide." *Kansas City Star*, 6 June, p. G-3.

Review of *The Bell Jar*. Summarizes the plot and mentions the mixed reviews the book received when first published in England.

18 HOLBROOK, DAVID. "Out of the Ash: Different Views of the 'Death Camp': Sylvia Plath, Al Alvarez, and Viktor Frankl." *Human World* 5 (November): 22-39.

Explores Plath's fascination with death camps by comparing it to the "work of one who survived a real death-camp," Viktor Frankel. Plath justifies "turning against her true self in the pursuit of a destructive purity" by creating the fantasy "of being a concentration camp inmate." Frankl's real death-camp experience, however, is exactly the opposite. He voices "concern with right action, . . . and with responsibility to be human, that can transcend "personal death, and find significance in 'having been.'"

19 HOROVITZ, ISRAEL. "'Some God Got Hold of Me.'" *Village Voice*, 28 October, pp. 27-30.

Considers *The Bell Jar*, Plath's "most revealing" work, a "roadmap" to her poetry. Briefly responds to Plath's suicide and to A. Alvarez's essay in his *The Savage God*. This article was published in two parts, the second in the 4 November edition of *The Village Voice* (A1971.20).

20 ____. "Success in Spite of Suicide." *Village Voice*, 4 November, pp. 21-22, 38.
　　　　A continuation of the article begun on 28 October (A1971.19).

21 HUGHES, OLWYN. "'The Savage God.'" Letter to the Editor. *Times Literary Supplement*, 3 December, p. 1525.
　　　　Discusses A. Alvarez's book, *The Savage God*. Maintains that although Alvarez has established himself as "*The* critic of Sylvia Plath's poetry," much of the material in his personal memoir about Plath is "speculation." Argues with Alvarez's "theory" that Plath's death was a gamble. Author gives her own explanation of Plath's "Death and Company" and includes a verse from that poem omitted in the final version.

22 HUGHES, TED. "*Ariel*." In *Poetry Book Society: The First Twenty-five Years*. Edited by Eric W. White. London: Poetry Book Society, pp. 33-34.
　　　　Reprint of 1965.B5*.

23 ____. "Commentary." *Times Literary Supplement*, 19 November, p. 1448.
　　　　Letter to the editor, in which Hughes discusses and takes exception to A. Alvarez's book, *The Savage God*. He accuses Alvarez of printing "fragmentary" facts and "speculative" theories.

24 ____. Letter to the editor. *Observer*, 21 November, p. 10.
　　　　Protests the publication of excerpts from A. Alvarez's memoir of Sylvia Plath on the grounds that he (Hughes) was not consulted. Alvarez responds in his own defense on the same page.

25 JACOBSON, DAN. "Mirrors Can Kill: Dan Jacobson Considers the Artistic Martyrdom of Sylvia Plath." *Listener* 86 (7 October): 482.
　　　　Review of *Winter Trees*. Suggests that in Plath's poems our common assumptions about the workings of an artist's mind are shown to be wrong. The common belief is that creative minds perceive reality "as ... harsh and obdurate." In [Plath's] work, the "principle is often [one] of Charity ... , while the inner world ... remains ... one of vengeance, ... bent upon injury to the self."

26   JENNINGS, ELIZABETH. "Poetry Selection." *Daily Telegraph*, 28
        October, p. 9.
              A review of *Winter Trees*. Presents the same "clear vision" as
        Ariel, but this volume has "more sadness" in it. The poet's "perilous
        state of mind" is also evident.

27   JOSLIN, STACY. "Female Insanity and Women's Oppression."
        International Socialist Review 32(June): 28-30.
              A review of *The Bell Jar* and *Zelda, A Biography* by Nancy
        Milford. The books are compared and contrasted. Neither is judged to
        be "feminist," yet both are "feminist in effect." *The Bell Jar* "chronicles
        the central conflicts of womanhood." Its heroine struggles to free
        herself from the exclusivity of the choices presented to her, and its
        author died in the attempt.

28   KEATING, DOUGLAS. "Four Poets: Brilliance to Sterility."
        Philadelphia Inquirer, 12 December, p. 204.
              A review of *Crossing the Water*. The poems in this volume may
        be Plath's best work because they were written after Plath "had
        matured as a poet but before she began to lose control of her emotions
        and, to some extent, her art."

29   KIRSCH, ROBERT. "First Novel also Her Last." *Los Angeles Times*,
        26 April, p. 7.
              Review of *The Bell Jar*. Disagrees with Plath's own assessment
        of the novel as a "potboiler." On the contrary, it stands on its own merit
        as a work of fiction. If Plath had lived, she undoubtedly would have
        gone on to write much better novels than this one.

30   LENSON, D. R. Review of *The Bell Jar*. *Panache* 7:51-53.
              Although the connection between Esther Greenwood's break-
        down and the 1950's culture is never "really explicit" in *The Bell Jar*, the
        "centrality" of the connection is obvious. The "drabness and
        conventionality" of the prose "is at the heart of the book's power."

31   MADDOCKS, MELVIN. "A Vacuum Abhorred." *Christian Science
        Monitor*, 15 April, p. 11.

Presents Plath as more than merely a "Dark Lady" of morbidity. Her emotional or mental problems did not prevent her from producing a remarkable amount of work in her short life. Instead of concentrating on her madness, readers should remember that what Plath "wanted, above all, was to *get out*" of the bell jar.

32   MAGLOW, T.O. "A Small Dissent." *Committee of Small Magazine Editors and Publishers Newsletter* 3 (December): 4.
      Expresses disdain for Plath's readers. They are often "bored intellectual women playing footsy with the notion of suicide. . . . [Plath] expired when young, and so she lights up all the dullest minds." Includes a short sarcastic poem that expresses the opinion that Plath's self-pity is boring.

33   MELANDER, INGRID. "Reviews." *Moderna Språk* 65:360-63.
      Discusses the interrelationship of the poetic themes and images in *The Colossus*, *Crossing the Water*, *Ariel*, and *Winter Trees* – especially "a mother's feelings for her child . . . , Plath's never-ceasing dialogue with death . . . [and] her headstrong defiance of the human predicament." Reprint of 1988.56.

34   NICHOLS, CHRISTY. "'Bell Jar' Sensitive, Truthful." *Lansing* (Mich.) *State Journal*, 3 April, pp. D-8, 9.
      Remarks on the importance of *The Bell Jar* as a "window into the world" of all tortured young people. It is similar to Salinger's *The Catcher in the Rye* in both tone and style; however, Esther Greenwood journeys far further into madness than Holden Caulfield does. The book stands on its own merits as a fictional work, "separated from the sad story of a real person."

35   O'HARA, T. Review of *The Bell Jar*. *Best Sellers* 31 (1 June): 123-24.
      Although the book is thinly disguised autobiography, Plath's style is "beautifully serene."

36   PETTINGELL, PHOEBE. "The Art of Dying." *New Leader* 54 (28 June): 19-20.
      Review of *The Bell Jar*. Includes a summary of the plot. The author "did not have enough detachment from her heroine to create a

true work of the imagination." The book is much better than most first novels, owing partly to Plath's skill at using fresh metaphors. Yet the suggestion that her work is interesting because "we are aware [of] her tragedy" cannot be dismissed or ignored.

37 PHILBRICK, STEPHEN. "The Life, Work, and World of Sylvia Plath." *Providence Sunday Journal*, 31 October, p. H-6.

Review of *Crossing the Water* and the reissued *The Bell Jar*. The *Crossing the Water* poems give an "order to many of the events and processes that so bewildered her in *The Bell Jar*. Occasionally Plath resorts to an "annoying vagueness"; at other times her style is "reminiscent of Emily Dickinson['s]."

38 POCHODA, ELIZABETH. "The Only Novel of the Dead Poet, Sylvia Plath." *Glamour* 65 (June): 119.

Review of *The Bell Jar*. The novel may have faults, "but it is superb in its faults." Much of its success is in the "simple and spare" narration of a "complicated and . . . highly dramatic" subject.

39 POWELL, DEBORAH. "When the Mind Becomes a Place of False Images." *Detroit Free Press*, 27 June, p. B-5.

Review of *The Bell Jar*. As the novel progresses, the narrator's voice becomes freer; "she has relinquished her desperate hold on sanity and writes with the brilliance of madness." The same can be said of the progression from *The Colossus* to *Ariel*.

40 RAKOSI, CARL. "Sylvia Plath: The Poetess and the Myth." *Minneapolis Tribune*, 14 November, pp. D-6,7.

Review of *Crossing the Water*. Many of the pieces are "nature poems," which reveal her highly developed powers of observation. In "quality of interpenetration they are akin to Wordsworth and early Edna St. Vincent Millay." However, sometimes she loses control of her emotions and "actively hallucina[tes]."

41 Review of *The Bell Jar. American Libraries* 2 (July-August): 762.

In addition to its autobiographical account of the breakdown, the novel paints an accurate picture of life in the fifties and offers "sparkling observations on the then-beginning sexual revolution."

42   Review of *The Bell Jar*. *Kirkus Reviews* 39 (1 February): 135-36.
          Includes a brief summary of the plot. The novel cannot be read objectively because of our knowledge of Plath's suicide. The writing is a "remarkable" example of "straightforward and irreducible simplicity."

43   Review of *The Bell Jar*. *New York Times Book Review*, 5 December, p. 82.
          Offers a brief description of the plot of this "single novel by the extraordinary poet who killed herself in 1963." Reprinted: A1971.44.

44   Review of *The Bell Jar*. *New York Times Book Review*, 6 June, p. 3.
          Reprint of A1971.43.

45   Review of *The Bell Jar*. *Publishers Weekly* 199 (1 March): 54.
          The novel "makes one ache for the loss of such talent and the personal pain it reveals." The heroine's slide into madness is told with "bitter wit . . . [and] harrowing candor."

46   Review of *Crossing the Water*. *Booklist* 68 (15 November): 266.
          These poems are death-obsessed, as is the use of the word *black* to connote death.

47   Review of *Crossing the Water*. *Kirkus Reviews* 39 (1 July): 727.
          These poems lend credence to the theory that "all . . . Plath's work . . . was a prologue to disaster." Her "single-minded purity [of] tone and images" point toward "her own annihilation." The *Ariel* poems are more remarkable, but *Crossing the Water* is significant in "recording her extraordinary development."

48   Review of *Crossing the Water*. *New York Times Book Review*, 5 December, p. 86.
          These are far from Plath's best poems, but they are valuable for showing her "progress on the way to *Ariel*."

49   SCRUTON, ROGER. "Sylvia Plath and the Savage God." *Spectator* 227 (18 December): 890.

Describes Plath's last poems, especially *Winter Trees*, as remarkable and surprising for their "complete avoidance of hysteria." Portrays Plath as a "craftsman," who displays a "deliberate striving for effect." Everything in both the *Ariel* and *Winter Trees* poems is "objective, concrete, conscious; we can feel moved by Sylvia Plath's obsessions without feeling any need to share in them." Reprinted: 1988.72.

50   S[IEVERS], S[HIRLEY]. "Recent Books for Hot Weather Reading." *South Bend Tribune*, 27 June, "Michiana" section, p. 11.

Review of *The Bell Jar*. The "pathos" is a result of the book's immediacy. The events happen "as the reader reads. It is not an imagined fear or imagined hell." One cannot ignore the impact on the novel of Plath's actual suicide.

51   STUBBLEFIELD, CHARLES. "A Craft." *Prairie Schooner* 45 (Spring): 83.

Reviews *The Colossus and Other Poems* and pronounces Plath "a master at her craft" who is able to make both small and large objects "vehicle[s] for ... significant statement[s]." Occasionally, however, she, like Frost, tries a bit too hard to get her point across. Briefly compares her to Auden and to Eberhart.

52   TANNER, TONY. "Interior Spaciousness: Car, Bell Jar, Tunnel and House." In *City of Words: American Fiction, 1950-70*. London: Jonathan Cape, New York: Harper and Row, pp. 260-67.

The Bell Jar is "perhaps the most compelling and controlled account of a mental breakdown ... in American fiction." It should not be discounted because it is rooted in autobiography. The main character's "estrangement from reality" makes her "a representative contemporary character."

53   TAYLOR, ROBERT. "Bright Journey into Night." *Boston Globe*, 16 April, p. 17.

Review of *The Bell Jar*. The tone of the novel is reminiscent of Salinger's *The Catcher in the Rye*. Although the story is bleak and dark, at times it contains a touch of "acrid humor." It is "harrowing" and "brilliantly authentic."

54 VENDLER, HELEN. "The Poetry of Sylvia Plath." Ziskind Lecture
Series, part 1, 13 December. Typescript at Smith College's Sophia
Smith Women's Archives, Northampton, Massachusetts, 23 pp.
States the purpose of the discussion as "to stretch out . . . some
of the elements of [Plath's] geography, to distinguish her in some
respects from her ancestors and . . . [poetic] peers, and . . . to
distinguish her final selves from each other." Traces Plath's "sense of
separateness" from her very early through final poems. The process of
shaping this "alien distinctness . . . into the vocation of poetry" can be
perceived throughout the whole body of Plath's work. Translated into
Spanish: 1974.26.

55 WELLS, SUSAN M. "Poet Tells Tragic End with Novel." *New Orleans
Times-Picayune*, 11 July, section 3, p. 9.
Review of *The Bell Jar*. Gives a brief summary of the plot and
concludes that the book is not "entertainment," but "art."

56 WOLFF, GEOFFREY. Review of *The Bell Jar*. *Newsweek*, 19 April, p.
118D.
Reviews *The Bell Jar*, proclaiming it a treatise on the
"inaccessibility of the psychotic." The novel is especially interesting
"because it was written by a very, very special poet." Reprinted: 1988.91.

1972

1 BANKS, NANCY. "Sylvia Plath's Sad Fury." *Chicago Daily News*, 4
November, "Panorama" section, p. 8.
Review of *Winter Trees*. With a few exceptions, the poems "lack
the sheer emotional impact" of those in *Ariel*. If this volume does not
contribute much to the author's reputation, it will at least put to rest the
argument over whether or not Plath was mad. Based on the evidence
here, she clearly was.

2 "Best Books for Young Adults 1971." *Top of the News* 28 (April):
313.
Review of *The Bell Jar*. Gives a one-sentence plot synopsis.

3   BOOTH, MARTIN. Letter to the Editor. *New Statesman* 84 (29 September): 433.

Reply to Eric Homberger's previously published article "The Uncollected Plath" (A1972.11. See also 1988.33). Corrects what he calls "several facts that [Homberger] is mistaken over and has not efficiently researched."

4   BRETT, ABIGAIL. "On Poetry and Poets, and Other Peculiar Things." *Houston Chronicle*, 29 October, "Zest" section, p. 14.

Review of *Winter Trees*. The poems confirm that Plath's "madness" has dulled both "her perception and her pen." She was dead as a poet before she committed suicide.

5   COATS, REED. Review of *The Bell Jar*. *Library Journal* 97 (15 February): 791-92.

Asserts that "Esther Greenwood is . . . Sylvia Plath." The reader is overwhelmed "with the aloneness of the narrator."

6   DAVIS, ROBIN REED. "The Honey Machine: Imagery Patterns in *Ariel*." *New Laurel Review* 1 (Spring): 23-31.

Attempts to disentangle "the [Sylvia Plath] myth from the criticism" and traces the origins of Plath studies, most of which have been "an orgy of tastelessness that discredits the artist and distorts and sensationalizes her art." Offers a "stylistic approach" to *Ariel* and concludes that the poet's biography is not essential to the meaning of the poems. Rather their meaning is built on "the overall patterns of imagery realized explicitly or implicitly in them."

7   DUKE, MAURICE. "Sylvia Plath's *Winter Trees* Will Not Change Readers' Views." *Richmond Times-Dispatch*, 1 October, p. F-5.

Characterizes the poems as "reflecting one of the most stark confrontations of the 'I' with the 'self'" to be found in recent poetry. However, this volume adds little to our knowledge of the poet. To make an informed judgment more of her work must be published.

8   ERIKSON, P[AMELA] D[ALE]. "Some Thoughts on Sylvia Plath." *Unisa English Studies* 10 (June): 45-52.

Focuses upon the lesser known Plath poems, primarily "The Stones" from *The Colossus* and "By Candlelight" from *Winter Trees*. Maintains that "'The Stones' shows Plath's style for the first time," and that "By Candlelight," unlike most of *Winter Trees*, is free from a "stark, brutal realism [and] distorted vision."

9   EVANS, NANCY BURR. "The Value and Peril for Women of Reading Women Writers." In *Images of Women in Fiction*. Edited by Susan Koppleman Cornillon. Bowling Green, Ohio: Bowling Green University. Popular Press, pp. 308-14.

Personal narrative which explains how Plath's *The Bell Jar* allowed this author truly to identify with literature for the first time and to "reconsider [her] approach to literature."

10   HOFFMAN, NANCY JO. "Reading Women's Poetry: The Meaning and Our Lives." *College English* 34 (October): 48-62.

Focuses on "Lady Lazarus" because it represents one of the few Plath poems which represents positive rather than negative changes for the persona. Yet when compared to Anne Sexton's "Live," "Lady Lazarus" is less affirmative because Plath's woman "tak[es] on the character of the enemy herself." Her images are bleak and repulsive compared with those of Sexton, who "presents a transformation" from a negative to an at least partially positive self-image. The article discusses both poems as they were presented to the class Hoffman was teaching and recounts the challenges her students made to her interpretation of the poems. Denise Levertov and Kate Chopin are also discussed briefly.

11   HOMBERGER, ERIC. "The Uncollected Plath." *New Statesman* 84 (22 September): 404-5.

Outlines the "random and piecemeal way" Plath is being published. Maintains that Plath, who was "the central poet of the Sixties," deserves the attention that an edition of posthumous collected poems would give her. Speculates on why there is no such collection. Reprinted: 1988.33.

12   HUGHES, OLWYN. Letter to the Editor. *New Statesman* 84 (29 September): 433.

Reply to Eric Homberger's article "The Uncollected Plath" (A1972.11. See also 1988.33). Announces that an edition of Plath's collected poetry is forthcoming.

13 KERTESZ, LOUISE. "More Plath Poems." *Daily Hampshire Gazette*, 16 September, p. 6.
      Review of *Winter Trees*. The poems explore the dark side of "woman as wife and mother." Some of the despair so evident in *Ariel* is explained in *Winter Trees*.

14 LINDBERG-SEYERSTED, BRITA. "On Sylvia Plath's Poetry." *Edda* 72: 54-59.
      Outlines the strengths and weaknesses of Ingrid Melander's study of Plath's poetic themes in *The Poetry of Sylvia Plath: A Study of Themes* (see 1972.A1*).

15 OATES, JOYCE CAROL. "One for Life, One for Death." *New York Times Book Review*, 19 November, pp. 7, 14.
      Review of *Winter Trees*. Contrasts it with Maxine Kumin's *Up Country*. Plath's book affirms death, while Kumin's affirms life.

16 P., C. "The Tragic Prophecy." *New Orleans Times-Picayune*, 4 May, section 4, p. 6.
      Reprint of A1972.19.

17 PEARSON, SHERY SHERMAN. "The Confessional Mode and Two Recent Poets." *Rackham Literary Studies* 2:1-10.
      Uses a reading of M. L. Rosenthal's book, *The New Poets* (1967. B11*) in order to re-evaluate the term "confessional poetry" as it is currently applied to Robert Lowell's *Life Studies* and Plath's *Ariel*. Concludes that the *Ariel* poems are not confessional and approaching them as if they were is "misleading" and inhibits understanding of her work.

18 PERLOFF, MARJORIE. "Extremist Poetry: Some Versions of the Sylvia Plath Myth." *Journal of Modern Literature* 2 (November): 581-88.

Questions the assertions made by A. Alvarez in his *The Savage God* especially as they are applied to Sylvia Plath. Does not accept Plath's suicide as what Alvarez describes as "an attempt 'to get herself out of a desperate corner which her own poetry had boxed her into.'" Any speculation about Plath is "safer" if done on the basis of her work. Such a study has been made nearly impossible, however, by Ted Hughes's chaotic, confusing, and scandal[ous]" publication of her poetry.

19　PETERSON, CLARENCE. Review of *The Bell Jar*. *Washington Post*, 30 April, "Book World" section, p. 8.

The novel is so engaging "that the reader nearly disintegrates" with the heroine. Reprinted: A1972.16.

20　PETERSON, HELEN R. "Poetry Reveals Melancholia of Its Author." *Albuquerque Journal*, 15 October, p. C-6.

Review of *Winter Trees*. The depression that eventually led to Plath's suicide is evident in many of the poems. In others there is hope, beauty and a sense of renewal. The volume ends on a positive note.

21　"Random Notes." *National Review* 24 (9 June): 650.

Notes the publication of *Winter Trees*.

22　REEVES, CAMPBELL. "Sylvia Plath's Final Poems." *News and Observer*, 2 January, section IV, p. 6.

A review of *Crossing the Water*. As in the rest of Plath's work, "it is impossible to separate the poet herself from her work" in this volume.

23　Review of *The Bell Jar*. *Best Sellers* 32 (1 May): 71.

A one sentence notice that calls the novel "haunting."

24　Review of *The Bell Jar*. *Library Journal* 97 (15 May): 1887.

The novel appeals to the same young adult audience as did *I Never Promised You a Rose Garden*.

25 Review of *Winter Trees*. *New York Times Book Review*, 3 December, p. 84.

Briefly describes the volume as the last one written by "'our acknowledged Queen of Sorrows.'"

26 SCHOTT, WEBSTER. "The Cult of Plath." *Washington Post*, 1 October, "Book World" section, p. 3.

Reviews *Winter Trees*. The poems do not equal those of *Ariel*. They are "depressing" and full of "suicidal gloom." The author of this collection was "a sick woman who made art of her sickness."

27 ____. "Flowers of Madness, Death." *San Francisco Examiner*, 13 October, p.39.

A review of *Winter Trees*. Attributes most of the "current adulation for" Plath to the fact of her suicide. The poems in this volume are not equal to those in *Ariel*. Reading them is exactly like being with "a truly emotionally ill person."

28 SERGEANT, HOWARD. "Poetry Review." *English* 21 (Summer): 75-77.

Review of *Winter Trees*. Although the poems are uneven in quality, all are valuable to readers interested in Plath.

29 SHOOK, MARGARET L. "Sylvia Plath: The Poet and the College." *Smith Alumnae Quarterly* 63 (April): 4-9.

Explores the relationship between *The Bell Jar* and Plath's actual experiences at Smith College. Suggests that Plath's portrait of Esther Greenwood "obscures the extent to which the real Sylvia Plath sought to become the perfect Smith girl." Neither does it show how much she loved her studies and appreciated her friends and mentors. Also examines Plath's early poems and suggests "connections between these" and her later work. Reprinted: 1988.74.

30 SHROYER, FREDERICK. "Moody, Rich Last Poems of Tragic Sylvia Plath." *Los Angeles Herald Examiner*, 1 October, p. E-7.

A review of *Winter Trees*. The poems are "rich, moody, genius-stuff, worthy of joining her other thin volumes of poetry."

31   SUK, JULIE. "Latest Poems Give Us Some of Plath's Best – and
     Worst." *Charlotte Observer*, 8 October, p. F-5.
          Review of *Winter Trees*. The volume "suffers by comparison to
     Ariel and *Crossing the Water*. The best selection is the radio drama,
     "Three Women."

32   WALLACE, ROBERT. Review of *Winter Trees*. *Book-of-the-Month
     Club News* (November): 7.
          Comments on Plath's "wit and power" as seen in these poems.
     Plath was certainly "one of the most significant poets of the last
     decade." Several of these poems are among the best she ever wrote.

33   WEST, PAUL. "Fido Littlesoul, The Bowel's Familiar." *Washington
     Post* and *Chicago Tribune*, 'Book World' section, 9 January, p. 8.
          Questions whether Plath would "have the standing she has" if
     she had "been ugly and not died in so deliberate a manner." Discusses
     the poems in terms of Plath's "unflagging sharp sensibility," and her
     tendency to choose a "precise look" in place of "hermeneutics."
     Reprinted with different title: 1984.42; 1988.90.

34   WHELAN, GLORIA. "Last Poems of a Dying Poet." *Detroit Free
     Press*, 24 September, p. C-19.
          Review of *Winter Trees*. Establishes Plath "as one of this
     country's finest poets." Instead of glorifying "self-immolation," the book
     presents death as cruel and vicious.

35   X., CATHERINE. "Sylvia Plath: Transitional Poems from the Gut."
     Los Angeles Free Press, 24-30 March, section 2, pp. 13, 15.
          A review essay of *Crossing the Water*. Comments that greed is
     at least partially responsible for the emergence of the "Sylvia Plath
     Cult." The imagery in this volume reflects a "letting go" of the
     "impersonal" and disconnected aspect of the language found in
     Colossus. The poet of *Ariel* begins to emerge in *Crossing the Water*, not
     in the first volume of her work. Plath "was the first twentieth-century
     woman poet who dared to be a woman, ... [to sing] a song from the
     gut, not from the head," and she sang it without imitating or seeking
     approval from "male poets and critics."

36   ZAVITZ, DWIGHT. "Tormented Spirit Found in Poetry." *News-Sentinel*, 9 December, "Weekender" section, p. 3.

Review of *Winter Trees*. This volume will earn for Plath the distinction of being one of the best of twentieth century poets. Writing poetry was a necessity for Plath, a matter not of choice but of compulsion. For readers who hold that "the purest poetry is written by a poet on the edge of existence, hanging in the balance between hope and despair, life and death, this book is a must."

Index

VAN DYNE, SUSAN, 1982.58;
1983.24; 1984.38; 1988.84
VENDLER, HELEN, 1971.B57*;
A1971.54; 1974.26; 1980.15;
1982.59; 1985.28
Viciousness in the Kitchen': Sylvia
Plath's Domestic Poetry,"
1977.14
Victoria Lucas and Elly
Higginbottom," 1985.7
Village Voice, A1971.19-20
Village Voice Literary Supplement,
1981.11
Virginia Quarterly Review, 1982.40
"Virginia Woolf and Sylvia Plath:
Inner Truths," 1976.55
"Vision and Voice in Three
Poems by Sylvia Plath,"
1974.23
"'Voice Hangs On Gay,
Tremulous, The,'" 1976.65;
1988.81
"Voices of Sylvia Plath, The,"
1982.33

WAGNER, JANET, A1953.7
WAGNER, LINDA W., 1977.55;
1981.28; 1982.60; 1983.25;
1984.39-41; 1985.29-30;
1986.13; 1987.10; 1988.87
WAIN, JOHN, 1961.B6*; 1988.88
"Waiting for Ariel," A1971.13
"Waiting for the Voice to Crack,"
1971.B36*; 1988.54
WALBURG, LORI, 1986.14
WALL, STEPHEN, A1966.15;
1988.89
WALLACE, ROBERT, A1972.32
WALSH, THOMAS P., 1974.16
WARD, DAVID, 1976.66
"Warnings from the Grave,"
A1966.13; 1970.A2*; 1988.78
Washington Post, A1971.3, 7;
A1972.19, 26, 33; 1976.38,

45; 1979.32, 35; 1981.9;
1982.8-9, 26
"Way Out of the Mind, A," 1982.3
WEATHERS, WINSTON,
1981.29
"Wellesley Club Awards and
School Letters Given at
Junior High School Final
Assembly," A1947.1;
"Wellesley Girl Found in Cellar,"
A1953.14
"Wellesley High School Students
Win High Honors in
National Atlantic School
Contest, A1948.1
WELLS, SUSAN M., A1971.55
WERNER, CRAIG HANSEN,
1982.61
WEST, PAUL, A1972.33; 1984.42;
1988.90
West Coast Review, 1973.12, 16
Western Humanities Review,
1974.8
"What Ceremony of Words,"
1985.22
"What Ever Happened to Mother
Goose?" 1976.38
Whatever is Moving, 1981.13
"What Have You Done? What
Have You Done?" 1983.3
WHELAN, GLORIA, A1972.34
"When the Mind Becomes a Place
of False Images," A1971.39
W[HITTEMORE], R[EED],
A1962.2
WHITTIER, GAYLE, 1976.67
"Who Was Sylvia?" 1975.14
WILHELM, ALBERT E.,
1980.16
WILL, NORMAN P., 1986.12
WILLIAMSON, ALAN, 1983.26;
1984.43
Wilson Library Bulletin, 1976.20
WIMSATT, MARGARET,
1982.62

DATE DUE

GAYLORD | | | PRINTED IN U.S.A